Reserve

D1512576

Springer Series

FOCUS ON MEN

Daniel Jay Sonkin, Ph.D., Series Editor
James H. Hennessy, Ph.D., Founding Editor

Focus on Men provides a wide range of books on the major
psychological, medical, and social issues confronting men today.

Ricardo Carrillo, PhD, is a Yaqui Mexican American currently serving as core faculty at John F. Kennedy University's Doctor of Psychology program and a clinical forensic psychologist in private practice in the San Francisco Bay Area. He has published previously in the area of family therapy with Latinos, sex offenders, and domestic violence offenders. He is the father of two children, Regina, 13, and Reynaldo, 12, a musician, and purveyor of the culinary arts.

Jerry Tello, is internationally recognized as an expert in the development of treatment, violence prevention, and community mobilization programs. He has extensive experience in the treatment of victims and perpetrators of abuse and in addictive behaviors, with a specialization in working with multiethnic populations.

Tello is the author of a Multicultural Fatherhood program, a Male Rites of Passage program, and a Domestic Violence Prevention/Intervention program. In addition, he has written for *Parent/Child, Early Childhood Today,* and *Lowrider* magazines and was recently featured in *Time, Newsweek,* and *People.* He is the author of a series of children's books and a master storyteller and trainer.

In April 1996 Tello received the Presidential Crime Victims Service award, which was presented to him by President Clinton and Attorney General Janet Reno, and in June 1996 he received the International Peace award.

He has been married to Doris Tello for 24 years and is the father of Marcos, 18, Renee, 12, and Emilio, 5.

Family Violence and Men of Color

Healing The Wounded Male Spirit

Ricardo Carrillo, PhD
Jerry Tello

 Springer Publishing Company

Copyright © 1998 by Springer Publishing Company, Inc.

Springer Publishing Company, Inc.
536 Broadway
New York, NY 10012-3955

Cover design by Janet Joachim
Cover illustration by Refugio Rodriguez
Acquisitions Editor: Bill Tucker
Production Editor: T. Orrantia

02 / 6 5

Library of Congress Cataloging-in-Publication Data

Family violence and men of color : healing the wounded male spirit /
   Ricardo Carrillo, Jerry Tello, editors.
     p.   cm. — (Focus on men)
   Includes bibliographical references and index.
   ISBN 0-8261-1173-4
   1. Family violence—United States—Cross-cultural studies.
2. Abusive men—United States—Cross-cultural studies. 3. Afro
-American men—Psychology. 4. Afro-American men—Attitudes.
I. Carrillo, Ricardo. II. Tello, Jerry. III. Series: Springer
series, focus on men.
  HV6626.52F55 1998
  362.82′92′08996073—dc21   97-51456
                                          CIP

Printed in the United States of America

In thanks to the ancestors and elders of the Mexican people who have taught, guided, healed, and supported me.

To CALMECAC and the Circulo de Hombres for their wisdom, ceremony, and "familia inspiration."

To all the healers and teachers of the world with a special acknowledgment and gratitude to those whose writings are shared here.

To Ricardo Carrillo, whose dedication to goodness and healing in the world has made this book a reality, and

To the circle of my family: my mother, father, brothers, sisters and to my "life teacher" and wife Doris, and to our children Marcos Antonio, Renee Amalia, and Emilio Alejandro, who collectively, are my reason for living.

El es Dios,
Jerry Tello

To Guadalupe Chavez who has demonstrated how to survive a lethal domestic violence relationship and still love herself and her children.

To Daniel Sonkin, Lenore Walker, Rosario Navarette, Michael Linzey, Hamish Sinclair and Antonio Ramirez, who all reflected in their own way, mentoring, direction, guidance, love, and challenge to stopping the violence among men.

To Yvette Flores-Ortiz, Concha Saucedo, Belinda Gallegos, Sandra Camacho and the many more women of color, who have supported us in our endeavors to write about the men who have taught us the language, spirit, and bedside manner to help them heal from the violence perpetrated on them and in turn, inflicted upon their families. Without the women's support, we would have not had the courage to have undertaken this contribution to the field of family violence.

Con todo cariño,
Ricardo

Contents

Contributors

Bonnie Duran (Coushatta/Opelousas), DPH, has spent over 20 years working in Native clinics as a provider and administrator. She completed her graduate work at UC Berkeley and is a professor at the University of New Mexico Medical School of Public Health. Her area of research has been in Native alcoholism. Dr. Duran's work has utilized innovative methodology in an attempt to find new and fresh answers to old problems in Indian country. She co-authored *Native American Postcolonial Psychology* as well as other related articles.

Eduardo Duran, PhD, has been working as a clinician, administrator, researcher, and theoretician in Indian country for 15 years. He has developed and implemented a rural Indian mental health clinic in central California as well as an urban clinic in Oakland and one in Albuquerque, New Mexico. He has written several articles in the area of mental health theory as well as the recent book entitled *Native American Postcolonial Psychology* which is co-authored with his wife Bonnie. Most of the theoretical underpinnings of Duran's work have to do with the legitimization of non-Western epistemologies as valid methods of clinical and research activity. Presently he is Senior Principal Investigator on a research project that is evaluating some of his theoretical work. Duran is also the director of Behavioral Services at First Nations Community Healthsource in Albuquerque.

Rolando E. Goubaud-Reyna, MSW, LCSW, was born and raised in Guatemala City. He obtained a degree in psychology in *Universidad do San Carlos de Guatemala*, came to the United States in the late 70s as a political refugee. He helped design and implement family violence treatment programs for primarily Spanish speaking adult male offenders in Denver, and in the San Joaquin and San Mateo Counties, California. While residing in San Joaquin County, he co-founded the *Hispanic Mental Health Professionals of San Joaquin County*. He obtained a MSW from San Jose State University. Currently he works for the Santa Clara County Mental Health Department providing mental health services for juveniles involved with the criminal justice system. Additionally, he has provided training on domestic violence for staff and interns with the Family and Children's Division of the Santa Clara County Mental Health Department, and assisted in planning and organizing two Latino Domestic Violence Conferences in Santa Clara County, California.

Robert L. Hampton, PhD, is Associate Provost for Academic Affairs and Dean for Undergraduate Studies and Professor of Family Students and Sociology at the University of Maryland, College Park. He has published extensively in the field of family violence and is editor of *Violence in the Black Family: Correlates and Consequences* (1987), *Black Family Violence: Current Research and Theory* (1991), *Family Violence: Prevention and Treatment* (1993), and *Preventing Violence in America* (1996). His research interests include interspousal violence, family abuse, male violence, community violence, resilience, and institutional responses to violence.

Joan Kim is a graduate student in the Department of Family Studies at the University of Maryland, College Park. She has research experience in homeless and other high-risk children, youth, and families.

Benjamin R. Tong, PhD, is Associate Professor, Division of Clinical Psychology, California Institute of Integral Studies, San Francisco; Faculty Emeritus, Asian American Studies Department, San Francisco State University; Research Associate, Institute for the Study of Social Change, University of California, Berkeley; Executive Director, Institute for Crosscultural Research, San Francisco; psychotherapist and consultant in private practice.

Lee Mun Wah is a 49-year-old Chinese American community therapist practicing in Berkeley, California. For the past ten years he has been the founder and facilitator of an Asian Men's Group and a Multicultural Men's Group dealing with racism, intimate anger, and the development of community leadership. He is a poet, filmmaker (*Stolen Ground* and *Color of Fear*), and director of Stir Fry Productions, which deals with the dynamics of developing a multicultural community in social agencies, businesses, and schools.

Oliver J. Williams, PhD, MSW, MPH, is an Associate Professor of Social Work at the University of Minnesota in Minneapolis. He is a practitioner as well as an academic. As a practitioner, he has worked in the field of domestic violence for over 18 years. He has been a child welfare and delinquency worker, has worked in battered women shelters, has created and conducted counseling groups for partner abuse treatment programs and has provided court-mandated counseling to sex offenders. As an academic, his research and published work centered on creating effective service delivery strategies that will reduce the violent behavior of African American men who batter. In addition, he also writes about ethnically sensitive practice, aging, and elder maltreatment. He has conducted training nationally on the subject of research and service delivery issues in the areas of child abuse, partner abuse, and elder maltreatment.

Pamela Woodis (Apache), MA, is a Therapist/Coordinator at First Nations Community Healthsource in Albuquerque. She received her master's degree from the University of New Mexico and her undergraduate degree from Fort Lewis College in Durango, Colorado. She is a member of the Jicarilla Apache tribe and has worked with the tribe as a counselor. Pam spent her early years living with the Dine' in Shiprock and her present work is serving urban Indian families and children who represent Indians from many tribes.

Wilbur Woodis, MA, is management analyst in charge of information systems for the alcoholism and substance abuse program branch of the Indian Health Service, which is a national program serving over 400 native tribes throughout the United States including Alaska. He is a clinician and does consulting with Indian agencies. Mr. Woodis received his Masters of Arts degree in Counseling from the University of New Mexico. He has worked with his tribal group, the Navajo, as well as with the Ute Mountain Utes, Southern Utes, Jicarilla Apaches, and Pueblos in the areas of community corrections, chemical dependency, mental health, education, public health and program development.

Foreword

Two years ago I attended a workshop on "Family Violence and Men of Color." The workshop was organized by Ricardo Carrillo and Jerry Tello, editors of this volume. It was held on the campus of John F. Kennedy University in Orinda, California.

When I walked into the conference room, it was apparent that this would not be the usual academic gathering. In the center of the room was a table on which were arranged various objects. The chairs for the audience were arranged in a semicircle around the table. Ricardo Carrillo welcomed the participants and explained that the objects on the table were sacred objects from various ethnic traditions—Native American, African American, Chicano/Latino and Asian American—and that they represented fire, water, air, and spirit. The table was an altar, he said, and the meeting was opened with a ceremony and prayers invoking the blessings of the Great Spirit and the ancestors.

It was a moving and powerful way to begin a workshop on a subject that is a source of trauma and pain. The opening ceremony projected a major theme of the workshop: Stopping domestic violence requires spiritual healing. That is also a major theme of this volume. Indeed, the panelists in the workshop—Ricardo Carrillo, Jerry Tello, Rolando Goubaud-Reyna, Oliver Williams, Eduardo Duran, Wilbur Woodis, and Benjamin Tong—are among the contributors to this book.

The advocacy of a spiritual dimension in halting and preventing family violence is a unique contribution of this volume. It is a perspective that grows out of the many years of practice in communities of color that are represented by the contributors. It is a perspective that grows out of the healing traditions found in these communities, traditions in which spirituality plays a central role. This is not to downplay the importance of issues of personal accountability and responsibility in treating batterers. It does suggest that accountability and responsibility are more firmly embraced when they are grounded in the varied spiritual and cultural traditions of the batterers' communities. Storytelling, rituals, and ceremonies can be important parts of recovery. Finding a healing connection with community spiritual values can be a transformative experience.

The rich and diverse essays in this volume incorporate current research and theory in the field of domestic violence. They also manifest the hearts and spirits of the contributors, their compassion for the victims of violence, and their determination to stop family violence by transforming individual abusers and exposing the systemic violence that has brutalized entire communities.

Family Violence and Men of Color: Healing the Wounded Male Spirit is a gift, an offering made in the name of the spirit of life.

ROBERT L. ALLEN
The Black Scholar at
University of California at Berkeley

Prologue

The dialogue of how men, women, children, and communities stay in balance and deal with pain has been a discussion in communities since the beginning of time. Maintaining the integrity and identity of a person, a family, and a community, in reference to the cultural and social ideals, has always been at the core of a community's purpose. With specific reference to males, their development and their specific relationships to their partners, this, too, has always been at the center of the community's development, particularly in transitional or "rites of passage" teachings. Along with the social and historical changes that have occurred in cultures and communities, there has come much transition, confusion, and, in some instances, pain related to imbalanced relationships. This area of domestic or family violence is of great concern in every community and culture, with each group addressing it directly and/or indirectly in different ways.

Interest in the study of family violence has increased over the last 20 years, and the academic researchers and practitioners in this area have expanded that interest, many times out of necessity, into communities of color. Intervention programs for family violence can be found in virtually every major city in the United States, with service delivery extending into rural areas. A majority of the clients served by these programs are people of color. Many substance abuse and mental health systems and social service agencies are faced with the dilemma of treating people of color while having little or no information on how to handle the language, cultural, psychological, ecological, or narrative geography aspects.

Much of the research, methodology, and practice approaches assume that "one size fits all" when addressing topics in the social sciences, especially in the field of family violence. The research goals and objectives for the 1980s, as published by the Family Research Laboratory at the University of New Hampshire, did not include the needs of communities of color. The philosophical presuppositions continue to be based on white male European, Western-oriented models. Emerging transcultural social scientists are developing models based on worldviews that are different from the mainstream Western European model. These include issues of identity, traditions, customs, and healing practices.

All of the selected communities of color for this text, Chinese American, African American, Mexican American, and Native American, are only a representation of the multidimensional subcultural communities of color. Although diverse, all these communities have a history of colonialization by white Europeans, which has had a significant effect on who they are as a people and the oppressive pain from which they are attempting to recover. The implications of these historical, political, economic, and social factors are so profound and significant that all the contributors, independently, have seen it necessary to discuss these issues in their writings.

Although much knowledge exists in the wisdom of the indigenous people of each respective community, little has been formally written from that perspective. Therefore, this book serves as an introductory text to the discussion of family violence, which has conventionally been a discussion of a Western perception of power and gender. When we take ethnicity into account, or other issues of diversity and oppression, the discussion becomes increasingly complex. One of the difficulties the authors have encountered in the writing of this text is attempting to transcribe a worldview, based on oral tradition, in a respectful, authentic way and in a Western written form. The dilemma of honoring the historical pain, suffering, and healing processes of a people and, at the same time, addressing these issues in a form and manner that social science practitioners can understand and utilize was a major task.

This text is an attempt to begin to address these issues.

Initially, contributors were solicited on the following criteria:

1. They were respected researchers or practitioners with significant experience in their respective fields.
2. They were respected in their particular communities.
3. They could articulate their experiences in written narrative form.

Many of the possible contributors contacted could express their valuable knowledge in oral tradition; however, requiring the written word excluded their participation. In addition, many "experts" in the field of family violence were too busy attending to their work to contribute to this text.

What we found is that the development of this book entailed much more than just the gathering of the writings of significant authors. It is more the coming together of healers, practitioners, and storytellers, from various roads, all attempting to respectfully represent their community's voice. Through the process, in an interesting syncretistic manner, we found the authors producing similar work, with parallel symbols, metaphors, and processes, but in a manner "unique to their peoples' way." In addition, the pain of having been colonialized was at the core of many of our discussions, therefore drawing similar conclusions and facilitating common themes. So interdependent was the writing process to the actual work that one author voiced his process of writing as "too painful to write," thus showing the interconnectedness between the authors, the clients, and their communities.

The authors echoed that this pain seemed to mirror the experience of the men in treatment, whereby they felt "oppressed" by the law and the social service agencies in their respective relationships and, many times, by the intervention processes that were supposed to help them. Conversely, these processes seemed to confuse, humiliate, label, and essentially "reoppress" them.

It became apparent that men of color were not familiar with standard therapeutic interventions and, therefore, had difficulty expressing themselves honestly and taking responsibility for their violence. It was found that the models who used culturally familiar processes that allowed the men to share and express themselves in open and honest ways made healing possible for the men, and for their families, as well. The men reported that the use of ceremony, attending to spirituality, and the use of culturally relevant approaches, such as libations, storytelling, humor, and the rewriting of their narratives within an oral tradition (music, poetry, sweat lodges, talking circles), allowed for integrated hope and healing. Finally, couching the issues of family violence in the historical, political vein of oppression allowed the men to see their journey as a choice between liberation or continued internalized oppression. At the same time, it was the consistent and unwavering view by all of the authors that family violence not only was unacceptable, regardless of past history or oppression, but was the antithesis of authentic manhood in "the traditional way." The end result is a reflection of the authors' diverse experience, utilizing experiential, existential, didactic, and narrative processes. The authors have attempted to include both theory and practice whenever possible, but obviously could not cover, in one publication, the totality of the issues.

We attempted to include representations of the Native American, African American, Chicano/Latino, and Asian cultures, realizing that this does not include the diversity of all cultures, or even the variations that exist within those cultures. It was our hope to initiate a dialogue, not as the definitive answer or end to the discussion, but merely as a contribution to a more inclusive reflection of the issues.

We have attempted to share in a good way, but if, on this journey through these writings, we have offended, such was not our intent. It was, and is, our intent to share, in hopes that we, as a people, can continue to heal and rebalance, thus creating a better place for the generations to come.

RICARDO CARRILLO
JERRY TELLO

Acknowledgments

The elders have taught us that life moves in a circle. So what appears to be new and original is actually just a journey of the circle revisited. In the traditional way, when a journey or new project was to begin, the entire community would gather in a circle and before any discussion of the journey would take place, there would be acknowledgments to the giver of life; to the four directions, the elders and teachers of that community. In like fashion we acknowledge

- The Creator, the source of all life and knowledge.
- The ancestors, ancient ones of all people who fought, struggled, and sacrificed for the dignity and good of humanity which allows such a writing to be shared.
- The elder teachings and gifts of the people of all roots which have contributed to the collective growth and healing of all people.
- Nana luna, Tonatzin grandmothers, mothers, sisters, partners, daughters and *all females: we ask your forgiveness. . . .* and thank you for your nurturance, support, teaching, healing, and perseverance in order that the children may have a better world to live in.
- The children who look to us for example, depend on us for protection and love; and rely on us to heal and balance their future world and especially . . .
- To all the children, women and men who have and/or continue to struggle with the pain of violence in their relationships, this book acknowledges you, in hopes that strength, support, and appropriate healing is forthcoming.

Introduction

Family Violence and Men of Color: Healing the Wounded Male Spirit is the beginning of an important journey, not the totality or the definitive answer to the dilemma, but a glimpse into another side of the dialogue.

This book begins with a review of the literature by Robert Hampton, Ricardo Carrillo, and Joan Kim on the major prevalence and incidence studies, to date, with communities of color. The authors describe, in a critical format, the difficulties with national reporting agencies and the implications of research methodologies with communities of color.

Chapters 2 and 3 cover the Chicano/Latino community. Jerry Tello's description of the Healing Tree and its connection to pre-Columbian teachings is significant in understanding and addressing domestic violence in this population. Ricardo Carrillo and Rolando Goubaud-Reyna describe their creative application of Tello's Healing Tree philosophy with Mexican/Central American immigrant men and their families in a way that demonstrates a balance between cultural sensitivity and clinical intervention.

In chapter 4 the African American community involvement with family violence is articulated by Oliver Williams in a theoretical, historical, and clinical application format. His approach is both scholarly and moving.

The Native American approach to working with men who are violent, substance-abusing, and suffering from intergenerational post-traumatic stress disorder is described in chapter 5 by Eduardo Duran (Apache/ Pueblo), Bonnie Duran, Wilbur Woodis (Dinee), and Pamela Woodis. Their discussion of postcolonial psychology and Navajo cosmology is the theoretical and spiritual basis for their approach to working with men in their community.

Chapter 6 begins with a wonderful, scholarly rendition by Ben Tong of Asian migration, colonization, and the impact of those issues on Asian men. In chapter 7, Lee Mun Wah follows in an impeccable manner with his unique style of helping Asian men heal from racism and violence in their homes. His clinical approach has influenced many practitioners in their treatment of domestic violence offenders.

The epilogue summarizes the significant lessons from each of the contributors and makes specific recommendations in reference to data collection, research, and treatment approaches that truly address and focus on the spirit and the needs of the respective ethnic populations.

There are many scholars and practitioners in the field working with families engaged in family violence. Additionally, there are many culturally competent authors and trainers. However, to have knowledge and be willing to share it in the written word is a blessing and a gift.

We would like to share those gifts with you.

1

Violence in Communities of Color

Robert Hampton, Ricardo Carrillo, and Joan Kim

Public and political attention to domestic violence has increased in recent decades. Discussion of rape and wife battering has become more prevalent in public media, and services for battered and raped women have become more available (National Research Council, 1996).

The societal dimensions of the problem are also now more clearly understood: Every year, an estimated 2 million women are battered by an intimate partner, and approximately 1,500 women are murdered by husbands or boyfriends (National Research Council, 1996). Nearly 29% of the 3.8 million assaults and 500,000 rapes sustained by women in 1992–1993 were committed by an intimate (U.S. Department of Justice, 1994). From 1990 to 1994, the number of reports for alleged child maltreatment jumped from 2,577,645 to 2,935,470. Of these, approximately 7.9 million cases (or 41%) were substantiated over the past 5 years (National Center on Child Abuse and Neglect, 1996). Once considered a taboo and limited aberration, family violence is now recognized as a prevalent social problem by researchers, practitioners, and the general public.

Violence and homicide in communities of color, especially in the African American and Latino/Hispanic communities, have also become a focus of public attention. Demand has risen for the prevention and control of violence in these particular communities, partially because of a growing realization that minorities experience disproportionate mortality and morbidity as a direct consequence of violence. According to the National Research Council's Panel on the Understanding and Control of Violent Behavior (1993):

- Americans of minority status are at greater risk of victimization by violent crime than are those of majority status.

- Blacks, especially Black males, are disproportionately the victims of homicide than are white Americans.
- Blacks are disproportionately represented in all arrests, and more so in those for violent crimes than for property crimes. In terms of violent crimes, Blacks constitute 45% of all arrests. They are most over-represented in the most serious violent crimes of homicide, forcible rape, and robbery.

From 1976 to 1993, Black males and females in all age categories had far higher homicide rates than their White counterparts (U.S. Department of Justice, July 1994). In 1992, the homicide rate (per 100,000) for Black males was 67.5, compared to 9.1 for White males. Black females had a homicide rate of 13.1, versus 2.8 for White females and 10.7 for women of color overall (National Center for Health Statistics, 1992). Overwhelmingly, Black males age 18 to 24 faced the greatest risk for lethal victimization: In 1993, the homicide rate for Black men age 18 to 24 was 184.1 (per 100,000), versus 17.4 for White men in the same category (U.S. Department of Justice, July 1994). These high homicide rates have led African American men to be targeted for classification as an "endangered species" (Gibbs, 1988).

Within this context, all types of violence in communities of color are a public health and criminal justice concern. As reported by the U.S. Department of Health and Human Service's Office of Minority Health (1994): "African Americans, the largest minority population in the United States, suffer disproportionately from preventable diseases and deaths." Street (1989) argued that, without a willingness to deal with race, "we cannot make headway in dealing with crime in this country" (p. 29).

The disproportionate representation of Blacks and some other minorities in violent crimes generally extends to intrafamilial violence, as discussed later in this chapter. However, despite the growing literature on family violence, recent research still largely ignores traditionally under represented groups and communities of color (Asbury, 1993; Hampton, 1987; Hampton & Yung, 1996; Huan & Ying, 1989). This omission not only limits the development of appropriate knowledge concerning the prevalence of violence among these groups, but also leaves practitioners without relevant information needed to develop culturally sensitive intervention and prevention programs.

This chapter examines previous research on lethal and nonlethal violence in an effort to better understand its prevalence, type, severity, and relationship to families. We begin by reviewing homicide differentials, child maltreatment, and spousal violence in families of color. We then examine approaches to data collection and research on families of color, noting any gaps or other research issues. Finally, we pose some additional issues to explore further within the chapters in this volume, as well as other research needs.

LETHAL VIOLENCE

Overall, intrafamily violence accounted for at least 18% of all homicides in 1990 (FBI, 1991) and 54% of all child homicides in 1994 (FBI, 1994).[1] According to a 1988 U.S. Department of Justice Survey of murder cases disposed in large urban counties, 16% of murder victims belonged to the defendant's family (Bureau of Justice Statistics, July 1994). Some general trends in family violence stand out in survey findings:[2]

- Spousal violence accounted for the largest share of family violence, representing 40% of intrafamily murders. In 1992, 18% of female homicide victims were killed by their spouse or ex-spouse, and an additional 10.2% by other relatives (FBI, 1992). Women were more likely to be victims in spousal violence cases, with 60% of the assailants in spousal murder cases being men. Women were disproportionately victimized in family homicide cases, comprising 45% of family murder victims, compared to a rate of only 18% for nonfamily murders.

- Although wives were more likely to be killed than their husbands in spousal violence cases, men still represented the majority (55%) of family murder victims. "Fathers, sons, and especially brothers are more likely to be killed by family members than their female counterparts" (National Research Council, 1993). Two thirds of assailants in family murders were men.

- Next to spousal violence, violence against young children was the next most common form of intrafamily murder. Fifty-seven percent of child homicide victims under age 12 were killed by their parents. Offspring represented 21% of family murder victims. Mothers accounted

---

[1]The Federal Bureau of Investigation's Uniform Crime Reports (UCR) system accounts for "most serious crimes committed" (National Research Council, 1993). The UCR conducts data collection on a national level of crimes committed in the United States. The UCR also collects additional homicide data through its Supplemental Homicide Reports (SHR). Homicidal data is codified from death certificates by the National Center for Health Statistics (NCHS), while nonfatal violent crime victimization reports are conducted by the National Criminal Victimization Survey conducted by the U.S. Department of Justice. In addition, the Center for Disease Control has attempted to tabulate homicidal data.

[2]Except when noted, all the statistics in the following list come from the Bureau of Justice Statistics, July 1994.

for 55% of the killers in such cases, and for the majority of murders of infants and small children, possibly in part due to greater risk exposure (National Research Council, 1993).

- From 1980 to 1994, children age 1 and under represented 45% of all child homicide victims, comprising the largest age group of child homicide victims (FBI, 1994). Newborns, infants, and children age 1 to 4 are at greater risk for becoming victims of homicide than are children age 5 to 9 (FBI, 1990, as cited in National Research Council, 1993). The majority (54%) of murdered children under 12 were boys (FBI, 1994).

- For murder victims age 60 and older, family members represented 27% of the assailants.

Many of these general trends in family violence seem to extend to African American families as well. Evidence indicates that partner homicide accounts for the majority of all lethal interactions among African American families (Plass, 1993). Similarly, in the aggregate, the most likely family murder victims and defendants were spouses, who accounted for 40% of family murder victims overall (Bureau of Justice Statistics, July 1994). Plass found that in African American families, boys are at higher risk for victimization than girls, while children under age 5 have higher victimization rates than do older children. Likewise, in the United States between 1980 and 1994, males accounted for 53.8% of child homicide victims (age 0–12), while children under 5 accounted for 72.1% of all child homicides in the same period (FBI, 1994). Plass also found that African American parents over age 50 are at greatest risk of being victimized by their children.

However, while some general trends in family violence seem to cut across race, the rates of intrafamilial violence have consistently been found to be higher for African American families than for White families. Intrafamily homicide rates have been found to have a high correlation with percent Black (.605) and percent poor (.560) (Williams & Flewelling, 1988). Overall, Blacks represented 54% of all murder victims in the United States, and 58% of all victims in family murders (Bureau of Justice Statistics, July 1994). Blacks comprised the majority of victims and defendants in spousal, offspring, and sibling murders, as indicated in Table 1.1.

Local and national studies (Block, 1987; Mercy and Saltzman, 1989; Saltzman et al., 1990; Zimring, Mukhjerjee, & Van Winkle, 1983) have also shown higher rates of spousal homicide among ethnic minorities (National Research Council, 1994). Based on 1976–1985 Supplemental Homicide Reporting data, African Americans comprise approximately 45% of spousal homicide victims, and have a spousal homicide rate 8.4 times greater than that of Whites (Mercy & Saltzman, 1989). In comparison to White women,

TABLE 1.1 Murder Victimization and Offending Rates by Race and Family Relationship, 1988

Relationship of Victim to Assailant	Race		
	White	Black	Other
Victims			
All	43.5%	54.2%	2.3%
Family	39.0%	58.6%	2.4%
Spouse	41.2%	56.4%	2.4%
Offspring	32.6%	65.6%	1.8%
Parent	54.8%	45.2%	0
Sibling	33.5%	64.5%	2.0%
Other	34.1%	61.0%	4.9%
Defendants			
All	36.2%	61.9%	1.8%
Family	39.7%	58.0%	2.3%
Spouse	41.8%	56.1%	2.2%
Offspring	34.5%	64.5%	1.0%
Parent	49.8%	50.2%	0
Sibling	32.2%	65.8%	2.0%
Other	38.1%	56.1%	5.9%

Source: Bureau of Justice Statistics, July 1994.

Black women face higher risk for intimate homicide (victimization by a spouse or boyfriend), even though the intimate homicide rate for Black women has declined over the past two decades (U.S. Department of Justice, November 1994). The intimate homicide rate for Black women age 18 to 34 fell from 8.4 per 100,000 in 1977 to 6 per 100,000 in 1992, while the rate for their White counterparts remained relatively constant. Currently, however, the intimate homicide rate for Black women (6 per 100,000) is still significantly higher than that for White women (1.4 per 100,000).

Black women are also more likely than their White counterparts to inflict lethal violence against their husbands. While 74% of White spousal murder victims were wives, only 59% of Black victims of spousal murder were women (U.S. Department of Justice, November 1994). The Bureau of Justice Statistics' 1988 survey of large urban counties found that Black wives were "just about as likely to kill their husbands as husbands were to kill their wives." This survey found that 47% of Black spousal murder victims were men and 53% women (U.S. Department of Justice, July 1994). However, proportionately larger numbers of Black wives are being killed than in years past: "In 1977, more Black husbands were killed than Black wives. . . . By 1992, fewer Black husbands were killed than Black wives" (U.S. Department of Justice, November 1994).

In a study of 12,872 domestic homicides occurring between 1965 and 1981 in Chicago, Block (1987) found substantially higher marital homicide rates among African Americans, and the lowest rates among Latinos. She found that while rates for marital homicide changed over time for each of the ethnic groups, the percentage of marital homicide (of all domestic homicides) remained consistent at 72% to 80% (National Research Council, 1994).

In addition to Block's findings, evidence from several other studies (Leyba, 1988; Rodriguez, 1988; Valdez & Nourjah, 1988; Zahn, 1988) indicates that marital homicide rates are lower among Latinos (Hampton & Yung, 1996). In particular, Zahn (1988) found that spousal homicide rates among Hispanics were lower than spousal homicide rates for African Americans and non-Hispanic whites. Using homicide data from nine cities, Zahn found that 47% of family homicides among Whites and 56 percent of family homicides among African Americans were perpetrated by spouses, while only 18% of Hispanic family homicides involved spouses.

Rates of lethal family violence against children also differed by race/ ethnicity. Black children were more likely to become victims of intrafamily murder than their White counterparts. The 1994 FBI Uniform Crime Reporting Program found that a disproportionate number (41%) of child homicide victims were Black (FBI, 1994). Within families, the risk for lethal victimization of Black children jumped even higher. According to the Bureau of Justice Statistics' 1988 survey, 65.6% of offspring murder victims were Black, while only 32.6% were white (U.S. Department of Justice, July 1994).

NONLETHAL VIOLENCE

As discussed above, minority families, especially Black families, experience a disproportionate share of lethal intrafamily violence. Ethnic differences in family violence incidence rates extend to nonlethal violence as well. In this section, we review research on the prevalence, distribution, and correlates of nonlethal family violence beginning with studies on violence toward children. Next, we discuss research on spousal violence.

VIOLENCE TOWARD CHILDREN IN BLACK AND HISPANIC FAMILIES

In the 47 states providing racial and ethnic data, African American children constituted a large proportion (26%) of reported victims of maltreatment, while Hispanic victims constituted 9%, and White families 56% (National Center on Child Abuse and Neglect, 1996). The rate for child maltreatment among African Americans was higher than for other ethnic groups, with Whites and Hispanics coming in second, and Asian/Pacific Islanders reporting the lowest levels of abuse/neglect. Based on national race/ethnicity estimates from the U.S. Bureau of the Census, the rate of child maltreatment among African Americans was 25 victims per 1000 under the age of 18; the rate for Whites was 11 per 1000; for Hispanics, 10 victims per 1000; while the child maltreatment rate among Asian/Pacific Islanders was only 4 victims per 1000 (National Center on Child Abuse and Neglect, 1996).

Elsewhere, parent-to-child violence rates among Hispanics have been reported to be higher than the child maltreatment rates reported by the National Center on Child Abuse and Neglect. Using data from the Second National Family Violence Survey (1985),[3] Straus and Smith (1990) found that the rate of child abuse 1 (kicking, biting, punching, beating up, scalding and attacks with weapons) as 48 per 1000 Hispanic children. The second measure, child abuse 2, adds hitting with an object such as a stick or belt of the items used in the first measure of child abuse. By this definition, 134 out of every 1000 Hispanic children were assaulted by a parent severely enough to be classified as "abuse."

Black children have been consistently reported as suffering from higher maltreatment rates. While they make up only 12% of the U.S. population, Black children represent 30% to 70% of all reported cases of child abuse in some regions of the country (National Research Council, 1993). Black children have also been documented as more likely to be reported for abuse/neglect in several national databases, including the Annual Fifty State Survey, conducted by the National Committee to Prevent Child Abuse (NCPCA, 1995); Westat's 1980 Study of the National Incidence and Prevalence of Child Abuse and Neglect; and the National Study on Child Abuse and

---

[3]This study was based on a national probability sample of 6002 households. The sample was drawn using a random digit dialing procedure and was made up of four parts. First, 4032 households were selected in proportion of the distribution of households in the 50 states. Then 958 households were over sampled in 25 states. This was done to ensure that there would be 36 states with at least 100 completed interviews. Finally, two additional oversamples were drawn—508 and 510 Hispanic households. The procedure for identifying the Black and Hispanic oversamples was almost identical to the procedure for developing the main sample.

Neglect Reporting (NRS), conducted by the American Human Association between 1976 and 1987 (Thomas, 1995a).

Comparing the rate of violence used by Black parents to violence used by White parents, Hampton and Gelles (1991) found that Black parents were more likely to report throwing things at their children and hitting or trying to hit with an object. This is consistent with other studies of disciplinary techniques in Black families that report Black parents using belts, cords, switches, sticks, and straps to discipline their children (Hampton, 1987; Johnson & Showers, 1985; Lassiter, 1987; Showers & Bandman, 1986). Black parents were more likely to use severe and very severe violence toward their children (Hampton, Gelles, & Harrop, 1989). Based on 1985 National Family Violence Survey data, the rate for child abuse 1 and child abuse 2 for Black families in 1985 were 40 per 1000 Black children and 197 per 1000 Black children, respectively.

Examinations of the specific nature of the relationship between race and family violence have yielded mixed results. After controlling for social class and community (county) characteristics in examining validated cases of abuse and neglect in Texas (1975–1977), Spearly and Lauderdale (1983) found that Blacks still had higher rates of child maltreatment. Other studies (Asbury, 1993; Hampton, 1987) have reported that controls for social class reveal no ethnic differences in family violence patterns (Hammond & Yung, 1994).

The differential rates of reported child maltreatment among ethnic groups may be partially due to racial biases in the mandated reporting system. Several studies have shown that at least in some instances children from poor and minority families are more vulnerable to receiving the label "abuse" than children from more affluent households (Daro, 1988; Gelles, 1982; Hampton & Newberger, 1985; National Research Council, 1993; Williams, 1989; Zellman, 1992). Using a sample of cases from the First National Study of the Incidence and Severity of Child Abuse and Neglect (NIS, U.S. Department of Health and Human Services, 1981), Hampton and Newberger (1985) found that hospitals tend to overreport Blacks and Hispanics and underreport Whites. For Black and Hispanic families, recognition of alleged child maltreatment almost ensured reporting to child protective services. Additional empirical evidence from this study shows that socioeconomic factors and race are as frequently or more frequently associated with child maltreatment reporting than the nature and severity of the child's injury.

Zellman (1992) found that socioeconomic status and race appear to influence report-relevant decisions, at least to some degree. In cases involving lower socioeconomic status (SES) and Black families, professionals generally judged the case to be more serious and more likely to be defined as abuse. The law was regarded as more clearly requiring a report. In such cases, the outcomes of reports were also judged to be better for lower-status families, and in every case respondents were more likely to report them (Zellman, 1992).

Other studies suggest that social factors may have contributed to racial differences in child maltreatment rates. Spearly and Lauderdale (1983) found that a greater proportion of high-risk families alone in a given area was responsible for increased rates of maltreatment. When combined with the presence of a highly urban environment, a great concentration of high-risk families in a given area may yield particularly high rates of maltreatment for Blacks relative to the majority population.

Spearly and Lauderdale (1983) and other researchers have suggested that cultural factors may influence differences in rates for particular types of maltreatment, even while they acknowledge the potential biases of differential labeling in accounting for ethnic differences in reported rates. For example, they suggest that the lower abuse rates among Mexican Americans suggests "less manifest aggression and violence toward children," which may reflect socialization patterns producing a "more passively and internally oriented style of coping with problems and challenges of life" and a personality type that is "more accepting of life's conditions and less aggressive in interpersonal relations" (Lauderdale, Valivnas, & Anderson, 1980). Caution must be exercised with this explanation because it is easily construed as merely restating a simplistic stereotype (Gabarino & Ebata, 1983). What is more, this explanation can lead to obscuring differences within Spanish-speaking groups (Laosa, 1979, 1981).

Other studies (Children's Defense Fund, 1993; National Commission on Children, 1991; Daniel, Hampton, & Newberger, 1987; Lauderdale et al., 1983) have pointed to environmental stresses, including racism and poverty, as factors leading to violent, abusive, and/or neglectful behavior toward children in African American families (Thomas, 1995a). Family turmoil can translate into victimization of children as parents take out their anger and frustration on their children in the form of physical or sexual abuse, neglect, abduction, abandonment, or even murder. Specifically, poverty can hinder parents' ability to protect their children, and can also hinder children's health and development, potentially leading to academic difficulties, delinquency, early childbearing, and adult poverty. Furthermore, community support from neighbors, community services, schools, and other public institutions has eroded, leaving families even more vulnerable to the negative effects of poverty and other external stresses (Thomas, 1995b).

Such external stresses also include drug and alcohol abuse, the most frequently implicated factor in the rise of child abuse and neglect (U.S. Advisory Board on Child Abuse and Neglect, 1991). Representing the fastest growing segment of candidates for foster care, African American drug- and alcohol-exposed children needing out-of-home placement are overwhelming the foster care system (National Committee to Prevent Child Abuse, 1992). Drug and alcohol abuse also contributes to community violence (Lynch & Hanson, 1992), which causes emotional damage to both caretakers and children (Thomas, 1995a).

The NIS data set (U.S. Department of Health and Human Services, 1981) provides other important insights on possible environmental stresses influencing child maltreatment rates. In comparison to Whites and Hispanics, substantiated maltreatment cases among Blacks included families who were poorer, more likely to be on public assistance, and in father-absent households (Hampton, 1987b). Nonwhite children were younger than Whites, nonwhite parents had fewer years of formal education; nonwhite mothers were younger; and Black mothers in particular were more likely to be unemployed. Compared to Whites and Blacks, Hispanic physical abuse victims were younger, more likely to be in father-present families, more likely to live in urban areas, and more frequently reported to child protective services by schools. Caseworkers reported that caretaker stress was associated strongly with physical abuse in general and to an even greater extent in nonwhite families. Among Hispanics, caretaker stress was cited as a factor contributing to abuse in over 51% of the cases (versus 40% for Blacks and 32% for Whites).

The rates of parent-to-child violence were higher for Hispanic and Black families than for White families. Because no comprehensive comparative analyses of these group differences have been conducted on these data to date, it is difficult to assess the extent to which these differences may be related to income, education, employment status, or other factors. However, existing data do suggest that such external social factors may in fact play a critical role in Black and Hispanic parent-to-child violence.

COUPLE VIOLENCE

Unfortunately, there are no "official" data on couple violence. In spite of potential for obvious biases, official data were they to be available would provide information on an extremely large number of cases known to authorities and service providers. In the absence of these data, researchers must rely on data collected in either clinical or survey samples. Official criminal justice data tend to underreport domestic violence against women, since nearly half of all domestic violence incidents found by the National Crime Survey had not been reported to the police (U.S. Department of Justice, August 1986).

COUPLE VIOLENCE AMONG AFRICAN AMERICANS

The U.S. Department of Justice reports that Black and Hispanic women, as well as never-married women in lower-income and younger age groups, were most vulnerable to becoming the victims of violent crime (U.S. Department of Justice, November 1994). Other studies (Cazenave & Straus, 1990; Hampton & Gelles, 1994; Sorenson, Upchurch, & Shen, 1996; Straus & Gelles, 1986) also indicate that African Americans report physical violence by intimates more frequently than whites (National Research Council, 1996). However, the revised National Crime Victimization Survey (NCVS), administered in 1992, found no statistically significant differences between ethnic groups in violent victimization rates by intimates. (This figure includes rapes, sexual assaults, robberies, and aggravated and simple assaults, but excludes homicides.) The NCVS did find elevated risk levels for violent victimization by an intimate among women with annual family incomes under $10,000 (U.S. Department of Justice, August 1995).

The First National Family Violence Survey (Straus, Gelles, & Stienmetz, 1980) is generally cited as the first comprehensive source of data on the prevalence and incidence of spousal violence in Black families. Straus and his colleagues reported that Black husbands had higher rates of overall and severe violence toward their wives than White husbands. According to the NFVS, the rate of severe violence toward wives, or wife abuse, in Black families was 113 per 1000, while the rate was 30 per 1000 in White households. Violence in Black families was more likely to be reciprocal: Black wives responding to the NFVS were twice as likely to engage in acts of severe violence against their husbands (76 per 1000) compared with White wives (41 per 1000).

The Second National Family Violence Survey (1985) was designed to address many of the shortcomings of previous research. A comparison of data from the two surveys revealed that overall husband-to-wife violence was unchanged between 1975 and 1985. Severe violence, or "wife beating," declined by 43.4%. Furthermore, these data revealed an increase in the rate of overall and severe wife-to-husband violence (Hampton, et al., 1989).[4]

Cazenave and Straus (1990) reported that when income is controlled, Black respondents were less likely to report instances of spousal slapping at every income range except the $611,999 level. Black respondents at both ends of the income scale were less likely to report engaging in these behaviors than Whites with comparable incomes. Cazenave and Straus (1979) noted that the persistence of higher rates of spousal violence for the large

---

[4]The comparison was based on the more limited version of the Conflict Tactics Scale.

income group containing the Black working class, and for Blacks in both occupational groups, suggests that even aside from income differentials, Black spousal violence is notably high.

Although statistics suggest that Black families represent a significant portion of violent families identified and served by agencies, this may in part reflect the actions of gatekeepers and not racial differences in the type, nature, or severity of family violence (Hampton, 1987; Hampton & Newberger, 1985). Cazenave and Straus's (1979) analysis of data from the First National Family Violence Survey seems to suggest that there is a need to examine further factors associated with spouse abuse among Blacks.

VIOLENCE AMONG HISPANIC COUPLES

Studies on the prevalence of physical violence in Hispanic marriages have resulted in contradictory findings (National Research Council, 1996). Straus and Smith (1990) reported Hispanics to be at greater risk than non-Hispanic Whites, while Sorenson and Telles (1991) found the risk levels to be similar. Sorenson et al. (1996) found lower levels of physical violence among Hispanics than among non-Hispanic Whites; likewise, other studies (Sorenson, Siegel, Golding, & Burman, 1987; Sorenson & Telles, 1991) found lower rates of sexual assault among Hispanic women (mostly of Mexican descent). Among Puerto Rican, Mexican, Mexican American, and Cuban groups, varying prevalence rates for wife assault were found (Kantor, Jasinksi, & Aldarondo, 1994).

In addition to varying prevalence rates, Kantor et al. (1994) also found that Hispanics as a group do not differ from Anglo Americans when cultural norms were held constant with wife assault rates. Nor can they be said to be a homogenous group, and finally the results confirm previous studies (Sorenson & Telles, 1991) that higher rates of acculturation are associated with an "increased risk of wife assaults by Mexican and Puerto Rican husbands" (p. 217).

Data collected as part of the Los Angeles Epidemiologic Catchment Area (ECA) survey provide us with the best studies of couple violence among Hispanics. To avoid problems associated with generalizing across Hispanic subgroups, analyses were limited to persons of Mexican descent. The sample included 1243 Mexican American and 1149 non- Hispanic whites (Sorenson & Telles, 1991).

There were no significant differences between non-Hispanic White and Mexican American families in lifetime rates of self-reported violence toward a spouse. Spousal violence rates for Mexican Americans born in Mexico and non-Hispanic Whites born in the United States were virtually equivalent (20.0% and 21.5%, respectively); rates were highest for Mexican Americans born in the United States (30.9%) (Sorenson & Telles, 1991). This research also revealed a gender difference, with women reporting higher rates of hitting or throwing things at their spouse/partner.

Perhaps the most important finding that emerged from this study was that rates of spousal violence among Mexican Americans vary according to immigration status. Mexican Americans born in the United States reported rates 2.4 times higher than those born in Mexico. This study suggested that this higher rate of violence may be in part related to cultural conflicts resulting from discrepancies between immigrants' familial culture of origin and the dominant culture in which they reside (Sorenson & Telles, 1991).

In a small clinical sample of immigrant families, Flores-Ortiz, Esteban, and Carrillo (1995) found a propensity to "freeze" particular cultural beliefs to maintain homeostasis. Specifically, patriarchal sex roles expectations were rigidified, leading to prevalent post-traumatic stress disorder, lack of open communication about specific issues (sexuality, previous pain with infidelity, and prior violent episodes), and an intergenerational transmission of the same frozen beliefs and attitudes to the next generation. The clinical issues described here are from an immigrant population and were found to be characteristic of families that have multiple problems, including family violence, alcoholism, marginalization, and discrimination.

FAMILY VIOLENCE AMONG ASIAN/PACIFIC ISLANDER AMERICANS

Data on family violence among Asian Americans is limited and fragmented (Chen & True, 1994). National statistics on Asian/Pacific Islander homicides combine suicide and homicide rates. These combined rates (per 100,000) for 15 to 24-year-old Asian/Pacific Islanders were 15.5 in 1987, 3.2 in 1988; and 17.5 in 1989 (U.S. Department of Education, 1992). A study of criminal homicides in Los Angeles (Loya et al., 1986) found that Asians accounted for a relatively small percentage (1.9%) of homicides compared to their population size (4.6% of the city's population in 1970; 6.1% in 1980). About 60% of these homicides were committed by strangers. Only 7.2% of homicides were committed by spouses or partners among Asian Americans, compared to 14.0% for whites, 17.2% for African Americans, and 5.4% for U.S. Latinos.

According to 1991 Uniform Crime Report data, 2.7% of families and children of Asian origin were victims of child or spouse abuse (FBI, 1991). Rates for child maltreatment and other forms of family violence also varied considerably among Asian subgroups (Chen & True, 1994). Reports for child abuse among Asian American populations in San Diego and San Francisco indicate a lower reported rate of incidence, especially compared to other ethnic groups; most of the reported Asian child abuse cases involved physical abuse (Chen & True, 1994). However, much Asian family violence may be hidden (Chen & True, 1994), as indicated by human service workers in the Asian American community (Ho, 1990; Lum, 1988; Masaki, 1992; Nakagawa, 1992; Rimonte, 1989).

ETHNIC COMPARISON

The Second National Family Violence Survey provides us with an opportunity to compare rates of couple violence for Blacks, non-Hispanic Whites, and Hispanics. This study found that Black and Hispanic families had comparable rates (174 per 1000 and 173 per 1000, respectively) of husband-to-wife violence. Whites reported lower rates of overall husband-to-wife and severe violence. The rate of severe assaults on wives in Black and Hispanic families, which can be considered a measure of wife beating, was more than double that of non-Hispanic White families.

Rates of overall wife-to-husband violence for Hispanic females were intermediate between those of Black and White females. Black women had the highest rates (207 per 1000) and White females the lowest (115 per 1000). A similar pattern holds for severe violence, where Black women had the highest rates followed by Hispanic and White females.

When broken down by male and female self-reports (male self-reports for offending, female reports of victimization), the 1985 National Family Violence Survey reports the following participation and offending rates for interpersonal violence toward women in the past year (see Table 1.2).

Again, African American men have the highest self-reported rates of violence toward female partners, While Hispanic men have the second-highest, and white men the lowest reported rates. The female self-reports did not differ significantly by race. Females were not more likely to report incidence of marital violence than men, although overall, females reported more severe and frequent abuse than males reported of their own behavior (Fagan & Browne, 1994).

The 1985 NFVS data also suggests that those engaged in severe parent-to-child violence were also more likely to perpetrate severe marital violence. There were also "no significant differences" in offending rates for severe marital violence across gender or ethnic groups, although African American males had slightly higher participation rates (Fagan & Browne, 1994).

Straus and Smith (1990) found that, compared to White families, the higher rates of spouse abuse in Hispanic families reflect the economic de-

TABLE 1.2 Self-Reported Offending and Participation Rates for Interpersonal Violence Toward Women, 1985

Race	Male Self-Reports of Offending	Female Self-Reports of Victimization
African American	17.1% average number of incidents: 4.3	10.7% average number of incidents: 8.6
Hispanic	14.1% average number of incidents: 3.9	14.4% average number of incidents: 10.1
White	9.7% average number of incidents: 3.9	10.6% average number of incidents: 6.8
Other	12.4% average number of incidents: 2.7	9.3% average number of incidents: 7.9

Source: National Family Violence Survey (1985), as cited in *Understanding and Preventing Violence* (National Research Council, 1994).

privation, youthfulness, and urban residence of Hispanics. When these factors are controlled, there are no statistically significant differences between Hispanics and non-Hispanic Whites.

Although income inequalities help explain differences in rates of violence between Black and White families, controlling for income does not exclusively account for the racial disparity (Hampton & Gelles, 1994; Hampton, et al., 1989). A number of additional factors must be considered in assessing domestic violence among Black partners (Hampton & Gelles, 1994).

A SECOND LOOK AT THE RELATIONSHIP BETWEEN RACE AND FAMILY VIOLENCE

As explained earlier, current empirical research has consistently shown higher levels of family violence and overall violent crime within Black communities, mixed conclusions for U.S. Latinos, and apparently lower rates of violence among Asian Americans. What accounts for the racial differences in rates of family homicide and other violent crime?

A closer look at the empirical evidence indicates that race is not as strong a predictor of violence as other social characteristics (Sampson &

Lauritsen, 1994). Sampson (1985, 1986) found that rates of violent victimization were two to three times higher in communities with high levels of family disruption, regardless of race. When he controlled for percent female-headed families, he found no significant relationship between percent Black and violent victimization (Sampson, 1985). Other studies (Messner & Tardiff, 1986; Smith & Jarjoura, 1988) also found that family structure, particularly percent single-parent families, has a much stronger causal relationship to violent crime rates than does race (Sampson & Lauritsen, 1994).

In their article for the National Research Council, Sampson and Lauritsen (1994) report that while rates of violence are usually higher in Black and/or other minority communities, "the direct effect of race is often quite weak" (p. 64). Residential mobility or change was more consistently correlated to violence, especially in the context of poverty, social dislocation, family disruption, and population density.

Similarly, while poverty is almost always strongly correlated with violence, it, too, has a weaker direct effect on violence than other community factors (Sampson & Lauritsen, 1994). When other community factors are controlled, the correlation between poverty and community violence becomes weaker. The crucial aspect of poverty in relation to violence seems to be "in the context of community *change*" (Sampson & Lauritsen, 1994, p. 63).

Overall, homicide rates in communities are strongly correlated with "population structure, resource deprivation/affluence, and percent of the male population divorced" (Land, McCall, & Cohen, 1990, p. 947). Resource deprivation has the greatest effect on homicide rates, followed by male divorce rate and population structure (Land et al., 1990). Housing and population density is another factor correlated with violent crime. Regardless of age, race, or gender, victimization rates were higher in high-density neighborhoods than in lower-density neighborhoods. The effects of density were independent of other community traits (Sampson, 1985). Another strong predictor of violence is family disruption, as measured by divorce rate or percent female-headed families. Block (1979), Messner and Tardiff (1986), Roncek (1981), Sampson (1985, 1986), Schuerman and Kobrin (1986), and Smith and Jarjoura (1988) have all documented the strong, positive relationship between violence and family disruption (Sampson & Lauritsen, 1994).

Similar correlations appear to hold true for intrafamily homicide. Fagan and Browne (1994) found "evidence that marital homicide is an urban phenomenon, more often located in social areas that typify the problems of urban areas: poverty, residential mobility, weak family structures, and concentrations of minority populations" (p. 176). Similar risk factors appear to be at work in both family and nonfamily homicides. The limited research on Black spouse abuse reveals similar variables, including occupation, income, embeddedness in social networks, unemployment, and violence in one's family of origin (Uzzell & Peebles-Wilkins, 1989).

Other studies also suggest a strong relationship between social disorganization and spousal violence, and the converse, between social stability and decreased violence. In their analysis of data from the First National Family Violence Survey, Cazenave and Straus (1990) found that embeddedness in primary networks is more closely associated with lowered rates of spousal slapping for Black couples than for White couples. For Black couples, the number of years in the neighborhood, the number of children, and the number of nonnuclear family members in the households were all associated with lowered levels of spousal violence. In spite of the small sample size (*n* = 147 Black families), these data provided some important insights concerning violence in Black families. The study revealed that a number of variables must be examined for a thorough comparison. The study also revealed that rates of violence among Blacks vary by family income, social class, and degree of social network embeddedness.

Still other studies suggest that marital violence among Blacks may be partially due to historical experiences of institutional racism. In assessing the effects of race on spousal violence, Lockhart and White (1989) and Lockhart (1991) found that a larger proportion of middle-class African American women reported that they were victims of violence by their marital partners than middle-class European American women. Using data gathered through a proposive sample in a large major southeastern metropolitan city, Lockhart argues that her data support Staples' (1976) conclusions that African American couples were not inherently more violent than European American couples. Higher levels of violence, when they do exist, may be due in part to the particular social predicament of African Americans in American society. By this reasoning, many Blacks have achieved middle-class positions only recently as a result of relatively recent changes in their lives and may have retained the norms, values, and role expectations of their lowered-SES developmental experiences (Lockhart, 1991). Aggressive and violent problem-solving strategies may be partially related to this background. Many African Americans are also subject to additional stress because of the uncertainty and tenuousness of their newly acquired position; this situation (i.e., process of adjustment to social change) may influence their use of violence.

In an ethnographic study of domestic violence against Black women, Richie (1996) proposed a "gender entrapment" model to explain the link between gender, race/ethnicity, social stigma, battering, and crime. In this model, social disenfranchisement conspired with gender inequality to "lure" Black women to seek respect and "success" in a socially constructed "ideal" nuclear family, only to be physically battered, forced into illegal activity, and then finally, incarcerated. Furthermore, she found these dynamics uniquely among Black women, and not among the White women in her study. Richie's model links hegemonic cultural values with social disenfranchisement (linked to both race and gender) in explaining how Black women become trapped within abusive intimate relationships.

Similarly, Lockhart (1985) hypothesized that socioeconomic factors accounted for racial differences in domestic violence rates. When ethnicity alone was taken into account, rates of spousal abuse were higher for Blacks. However, when SES among Blacks and Whites was controlled, the spousal abuse rate for Whites was equal to that of Blacks. One possible hypothesis explaining these results is that rates of violence change as a result of the level of poverty. Most poverty-level Whites do not fall into the category of "extreme poverty" that some Blacks do; therefore, comparison rates are misleading.

Risk factors for violent crime like social isolation and concentration effects are more commonly found in high-poverty, disproportionately Black urban areas. As argued by Wilson (1987), poor Blacks—especially female-headed families with children—have been increasingly isolated and disproportionately concentrated in inner-city areas. These communities have suffered the heaviest blows from structural economic changes resulting from the shift from goods-producing to service-producing industries: loss of manufacturing jobs and increasing gaps between high-wage and low-wage jobs. The loss of manufacturing jobs led to increased joblessness among Black males and persistent poverty, which in turn disrupted Black family structure in inner-city communities. Furthermore, Wilson argued, "social buffers"—institutions like churches, schools, stores, and recreational facilities—suffered as a result of the exodus of middle- and upper-income Black families from inner-city areas. With the loss of economically and socially stable families and with the disruption of remaining families, informal social controls and economic and social supports for communities weakened considerably. Family and social disruption became concentrated in communities that were increasingly isolated from the mainstream social and economic structures. Hypothetically, this concentrated social and family disruption led to increased violence in predominantly Black inner-city communities (Sampson, 1987).

This concentration of poverty has largely fallen along racial lines, taking a greater toll on Black than White communities and families. In 1980 in the five largest U.S. central cities, 70% of poor Whites lived in nonpoverty areas, compared to only 15% of poor Blacks. Only 7% of Whites lived in areas of extreme poverty, while nearly 40% of poor Blacks lived in such extreme-poverty areas (Sampson and Lauritsen, 1994). As a result, the typical residential community for a poor Black family differs significantly from that of a poor White family (Sampson, 1987; Stark, 1987). Even the "worst" White residential communities are significantly better off with respect to poverty and family disruption than the average Black community (Sampson, 1987). Consequently, according to Sampson & Lauritsen (1994),

> [t]he relationship between race and violence may be accounted for largely by community context (e.g., segregation, concentration of family disruption and joblessness, social isolation, sparse social networks). We simply do not know, and cannot know, given the typical individual-level research design. (p. 83)

Thus, a closer look at the empirical evidence suggests that social instability and change within a community have more to do with violent crime than race or even poverty. Race and poverty have both been found to have a strong correlation with violent crime, particularly homicide, but they appear to have become confounded with other social variables, such as family disruption, embeddedness in social networks, residential mobility, population/housing density, and the presence or absence of social organization in the surrounding community. Community characteristics, not just individual family characteristics, appear to have a significant impact on the risk for victimization by violent crime. Such family and community-level risk factors are more prevalent among urban minority, particularly African American, communities. The research in minority family violence also suggests that family violence, in particular, is sensitive to social influence such as the availability of social networks, resource deprivation, divorce rate, immigration status, and other forms of family or social disruption. Both family and nonfamily violence rates differ significantly by race; both types of violence also seem to be affected similarly by social context.

DATA COLLECTION AND RESEARCH ON FAMILIES OF COLOR

The relationship between race and family violence has been demonstrated, but the exact nature of this relationship and the causal variables involved are not as clearly understood. More research—especially methodologically different types of research—needs to be done to address the social processes and community-level characteristics that engender violence (Sampson & Lauritsen, 1994). Simple continuation of current research trends is insufficient for uncovering these social processes (Fingerhut & Kleinman, 1990). Current knowledge of minority family violence is limited due to weaknesses in data collection efforts, methodologies, and research perspectives that often fail to account for the complex social interactions leading to elevated levels of violence in minority families.

DATA COLLECTION NEEDS

Overall, there is a paucity of methodologies for data collection for viewing families of color. To date, there has been relatively little research or data collection on violence within families of color (National Research Council, 1996). National crime statistics collected by the Federal Bureau of Investigation and the National Center for Health Statistics generally classify victims as Black, White, and "Other"; consequently, there is no national homicide data for non–African American minority communities.

Families of color have been victims of benign neglect in community-based studies of spousal violence. While some studies on domestic violence include large numbers of African Americans and/or Hispanics, most concentrate on White families. The First National Family Violence Survey (Straus, et al., 1980) was constrained by the small sample of Black families ($n = 147$) and limited sampling frame. The survey did not include Hispanic families in sufficient numbers for comparative analyses. Although Asian Americans represent the fastest growing minority group in the U.S. (LaFromboise, 1992), the National Research Council (1996) found no survey studies of intimate violence experienced by Asian-American women. In particular, current research remains unclear on the influence of socioeconomic and cultural factors on racial differences in the self-reported incidence of physical violence between intimates (National Research Council, 1996).

Existing studies of minority family violence frequently lack culturally sensitive data collection methodologies. Although the Second National Family Violence Survey (1985) has contributed to the knowledge of family violence in Hispanic families, it also illustrates the lack of appropriate methodologies for the study of violent behavior in the Hispanic/Latino home. The survey was conducted by random digit dialing procedure, which accessed only those Hispanic households that had telephones. The survey was conducted in English, excluding any monolingual Spanish-speaking households (Straus & Gelles, 1990). In addition to ignoring the primary language of a large majority of the sample, it is questionable whether or not the forced choice responses were a result of a clear understanding of the questions asked.

Straus and Smith's (1989) study also ignores class, SES, and intragroup differences. An additional glaring omission is a measure of acculturation, and the impact of this variable on the questions asked and the type of response by the subject. The forced choice format of the survey limited the qualifying responses to quantifiable data. This study clearly demonstrates the difficulty with data collection methodologies and brings into question the high incidence and prevalence rates of Hispanic families. However, some of the same problems do not seem to apply to African American samples.

Research with Hispanic populations indicates that random digit dialing can be effective if conducted with same-language solicitors if the questions are presented in a culturally relevant manner (Marin, Sabogal, Marin, Otero, Sabogal, & Perez-Stable, 1986). Methodology is not as much a problem as the lack of cultural sensitivity in conducting research with Hispanic and other minority populations. Research in communities of color must take these communities' worldviews and cultures, as well as the process of acculturation, into consideration. Unfortunately, current research on domestic violence generally lacks the perspectives of women of color in research and instrument design. As explained by the National Research Council (1996):

> Most studies have used measures and instruments developed on Anglos and simply applied them to members of other ethnic groups, for whom the instruments' validity is unknown. There may be differences in the intent of a question and a respondent's interpretation related to patterns of expression and idioms that may vary across cultures. This may explain, in part, the lack of consistency of results across studies. (p. 42)

Gaps also exist in current research on child abuse and neglect in families of color. There is a need for "national case-specific data on issues of causation, consequences, and the prospects of child abuse/neglect in the African American community. There is also a need for empirical data explaining the influence of socioeconomic forces on abusive/neglectful behavior, and explaining the disproportionate representation of African American families within the foster care system (Thomas, 1995a, pp. 32–33). Samples and methodologies across studies also tend to be inconsistent, making it difficult to determine risk for family sexual abuse among African American youth (Asbury, 1993). Furthermore, traditional clinical research methodology of child abuse/neglect in families of color has suffered from biased or skewed sampling methodologies; insensitive subject recruitment strategies; and a general failure to address socioeconomic, cultural, and racial factors (Urquiza & Wyatt, 1994).

Inconsistent protocols for data collection efforts across national clearinghouses also make it difficult to draw reliable conclusions about minority family violence. For example, during the 1970s, the Uniform Crime Report (UCR) changed the criteria for data collection with respect to Spanish origin

and Spanish-speaking populations. As a result, the number of Hispanics involved in violent crimes as either offenders or victims increased by 33%.
Operational definitions may also differ across studies. For example, the National Crime Survey does not employ the commonly used Conflict Tactics
Scales,[5] but uses items that correspond with the UCR categories. As a result,
comparison rates are limited to "aggregate indices of violence and do not
address severity or specific acts" (National Research Council, 1994).

RESEARCH PERSPECTIVES

Not only is current literature on minority family violence limited by insufficient and/or inconsistent data collection, it is also limited by a defi-
ciency in culturally sensitive research perspectives. Research methods that
view the world from a Western European perspective and that minimize
the importance of collecting data from communities of color seem to assume deviancy and pathologize the rates of violence among communities
of color.

Up to recent times, conceptual models for the study of Black families in
particular have been heavily influenced by schools of thought that use the
traditional White middle-class family as the primary referent and that
view differences as "deviancy" or "pathology." Such a "pathologist" approach became particularly influential in the 1960s and 1970s with the
publication of Daniel Patrick Moynihan's report (1965) on Black families.
Moynihan targeted family disorganization as the principal cause of dete-
rioration in the Black community and "initiated the study of the Black
family as a pathological form of social organization" (Staples & Johnson,
1993).

Since that time, while the "pathologist" approach has remained influential, other research approaches for studying families of color have emerged.
In social science literature, differences between White middle-class families
and African American families have been explained recently in terms of cultural deviant, cultural equivalent, or cultural variant perspectives (Allen,
1978; Fine, Schwebel, & James-Myers, 1987). These perspectives are easily
extended to other families of color.

Researchers holding the cultural deviant perspective recognize that families of color are different from majority-group families. These differences

---

[5]The Conflict Tactics Scales (CTS), developed by M. A. Straus in 1978, "became the most consistent instrument for assessing the types of violence that occur between couples and their
frequency." The CTS constitutes the "baseline for providing epidemiological estimates and
comparisons across samples" (National Research Council, 1994).

are viewed, however, as deviancy, implying that the values and lifestyles of families of color are pathological. Quality of life for families is viewed through the values of mainstream culture, which often ignores the positive features of families of color.

The cultural equivalent perspective holds that there is no clear cultural distinction between majority families and families of color. Advocates of this perspective argue that differences in socioeconomic status, especially higher rates of poverty among many minority groups, explain group differences in family life. During the 1970s, research shifted predominantly to this perspective (Johnson, 1988).

The cultural variant perspective, which is largely evident in predominantly Black journals, argues that families of color are culturally unique, yet functional and legitimate (Staples & Johnson, 1993). One version of this position holds that among African Americans, the African cultural heritage is viewed as the primary determinant of family behavior. The conditions that African Americans encounter in the United States influence the expression and development of this basic African core (Fine et al., 1987). Similar to an ecological perspective, the cultural variant perspective recognizes the impact of differences in environments, which result in differences both in family structure and in ways of functioning. These family patterns are often necessary adaptations of a group culture to a new set of circumstances.

There is a danger of viewing all differences as healthy, when in fact some differences are pathological (Daniel, 1985). It must be understood that not all adaptations are positive and that to some extent the interpersonal violence we see in many communities of color may reflect negative adaptations.

CONCLUSION

The current literature indicates relatively higher levels of violence within African American families, a mixed set of study conclusions for Latino families, and little knowledge of the incidence or etiology of violence within Native American or Asian American/Pacific Islander families. African American families have consistently been reported to have higher incidence rates of lethal and nonlethal marital and parent-to-child violence. However, the socioeconomic factors implicated in these phenomena are not clearly understood. Large gaps in data exist concerning family violence among all minority communities, in part because of neglect or misunderstanding by the research community, in part because of language and cultural barriers. Because of the sensitive nature of family violence, all forms of family violence, particularly marital violence, tend to be underreported

(Bureau of Justice Statistics, 1988, 1993). A lack of culturally sensitive research and data collection methods, a lack of community-level measurement, as well as possible racial biases within the child welfare system and/or other public institutions, also cloud the picture and make conclusive findings difficult to draw.

Research methodologies must reflect the diversity of worldviews and reanalyze data that most notably account for differences from a nonpathological perspective. More sophisticated analyses are needed to explore the complicated variables of race/ethnicity, social class, culture, social networks, acculturation, and community-wide variables such as resource deprivation, residential turnover, family disruption, and other socioeconomic factors and their relationship to family violence. Future research should seek to recognize cultural differences in family functioning without viewing such differences as "deviant" or pathological, and should recognize the complex nature of differences between and within ethnic groups. Furthermore, future research should seek to address the large gaps in knowledge concerning violence among families of color, which have been understudied in years past.

While family violence remains tragic for all involved, minority families bear a disproportionately large share of the burden. More concentrated and culturally sensitive research can lead to a clearer understanding of the scope and causes of violence in families of color, which can in turn lead to more effective prevention and intervention efforts in years to come.

REFERENCES

Allen, W. R. (1978).The search for applicable theories of black family life. *Journal of Marriage and the Family, 40,* 117–129.

Asbury, J. (1993). Violence in families of color in the United States. In R. L. Hampton, T. Gullotta, G. R. Adams, E. Potter, and R. P. Weissberg, (Eds.), *Family Violence: Prevention and Treatment* (pp. 159–178). Newbury Park, CA: Sage.

Block, C. R. (1987, November). *Lethal violence at home: Racial/ethnic differences in domestic homicide in Chicago, 1965 to 1981.* Paper presented at the meeting of the American Society of Criminology, Chicago.

Block, R. (1979). Community, environment, and violent crime. *Criminology, 17,* 46–57.

Bureau of Justice Statistics. (1988). *Preventing domestic violence against women* (Special Report). Washington, DC: US Department of Justice Office of Justice Programs.

Bureau of Justice Statistics. (1993). *Murder in families.* (Special Report). Washington, DC: US Department of Justice Office of Justice Programs.

Cazenave, N. A. & Straus, M. A. (1990). Race, class, network embeddedness, and family violence: A search for potent support systems. *Journal of Comparative Family Studies, 10,* 281–299.

Chen, S. A. & True, R. H. (1994). Asian Americans. In L. D. Eron, J. H. Gentry, and P. Schlegel, (Eds.), *Reason to hope: A psychosocial perspective on violence and youth.* Washington, DC: American Psychological Association.

Children's Defense Fund. (1993). *Progress and peril: Black children in America.* The Black Community Crusade for Children.

Daniel, J. H. (1985). Cultural and ethnic issues: The black family. In E. H. Newberger and R. Bourne (Eds.), *Unhappy families* (pp. 145–153). Littleton, MA: PSG.

Daniel, J. H., Hampton, R. L., & Newberger, E. H. (1987). Child abuse and accidents in black families: A controlled comparative study. In R. L. Hampton (Ed.), *Violence in the black family: Correlates and consequences* (pp. 645–653). Lexington, MA: Lexington Books.

Daro, D. (1988). *Confronting child abuse.* New York: Free Press.

Fagan, J., & Browne, A. (1994). Violence between spouses and intimates: Physical aggression between women and men in intimate relationships. In National Research Council, *Understanding and preventing violence: Vol. 3. Social influences* (pp. 115–260). Washington, DC: National Academy Press.

Fine, M., Schwebel, A. I., & James-Myers, L. (1987). Family stability in black families: Values underlying three different perspectives. *Journal of Comparative Families Studies, 18,* 1–23.

Fingerhut, L., & Kleinman, J. (1990). International and interstate comparisons of homicide among young males. *Journal of the American Medical Association, 263,* 3292–3295.

Flores-Ortiz, Y., Esteban, M., & Carrillo, R. A. (1995). La Violencia en la familia: Un modelo contextual de terapia intergeneracional. *Revista InterAmericana de Psicologia/InterAmerican Journal of Psychology, 28*(2), pp 235–250.

Gabarino, J., & Ebata, A. (1983). The significance of ethnic and cultural differences in child maltreatment. *Journal of Marriage and the Family, 45,* 773–783.

Gelles, R. J. (1982). Child abuse and family violence: Implications for medical professionals. In E. H. Newberger (Ed.), *Child abuse* (pp. 25–42). Boston: Little, Brown.

Gibbs, J. T. (1988). *Young, black, and male in America: An endangered species.* Dover, MA: Auburn House.

Hammond, W. R., & Yung, B. R. (1994). African Americans. In L. D. Eron, J. H. Gentry, and P. Schlegel, (Eds). *Reason to hope: A psychosocial perspective on violence and youth.* Washington, DC: American Psychological Association.

Hampton, R. L. (1987a). Family violence and homicides in the black community: Are they linked? In R. L. Hampton (Ed.), *Violence in the black family: Correlates and consequences* (pp. 135–156). Lexington, MA: Lexington Books.

Hampton, R. L. (1987b). Violence against black children: Current knowledge and future research needs. In R. L. Hampton (Ed.), *Violence in the black family: Correlates and consequences* (pp. 3–20, 135–156). Lexington, MA: Lexington Books.

Hampton, R. L., & R. J. Gelles. (1991). A profile of violence toward black children. In R. L. Hampton (Ed.), *Black family violence: Current research and theory* (pp. 21–34). Lexington, MA: Lexington Books.

Hampton, R. L., & Gelles, R. J. (1994). Violence toward black women in a nationally representative sample of black families. *Journal of Comparative Family Studies, 25*(1), 105–119.

Hampton, R. L., Gelles, R. J., & Harrop, J. W. (1989). Is violence in black families increasing? A comparison of 1975 and 1985 national survey rates. *Journal of Marriage and the Family, 51,* 969–980.

Hampton, R. L., & Newberger, E. H. (1985). Child abuse incidence and reporting by hospitals: The significance of severity, class, and race. *American Journal of Public Health, 75,* 56–60.

Hampton, R. L., & Yung, B. R. (1996). Violence in communities of color: Where we were, where we are, and where we need to be. In R. L. Hampton, P. Jenkins, & T. Gullotta (Eds.), *Preventing violence in America* (pp. 53–86). Thousand Oaks, CA: Sage Publications.

Ho, C. (1990). An analysis of domestic violence in Asian American communities. *Women and Therapy, 9*(1–2), 129–150.

Huang, L. N. & Ying, Y.-W. (1989). Chinese-American children and adolescents. In J. T. Gibbs, L. N. Huang, et al. (Eds.), *Children of color* (pp. 30–66). San Francisco: Jossey- Bass.

Johnson, C. F., & Showers, J. (1985). Injury variables in child abuse. *Child Abuse and Neglect, 9,* 207–216.

Johnson, L. B. (1988). Perspectives on black family empirical research, 1965–1978. In H. P. McAdoo (Ed.), *Black families*(2nd ed.). Newbury Park, CA: Sage.

Kantor, G. K., Jasinski, J. L., & Aldarondo, E. (1994). Sociocultural status and incidence of marital violence in Hispanic families. *Violence and Victims 9*(3), 207–222.

LaFromboise, T. D. (1992). In obligation to our people: Giving merit to cultural and individual differences. *Focus 6*(1), 11–14.

Land, K., McCall, P. & Cohen, L. (1990). Structural covariates of homicide rates: Are there any invariances across time and space? *American Journal of Sociology, 95,* 922–963.

Lassiter, R. F. (1987). Child rearing in black families: Child-abusing discipline. In R. L. Hampton (Ed.), *Violence in the black family: Correlates and consequences* (pp. 3–20). Lexington, MA: Lexington Books.

Laosa, L. M. (1979). Social competence in childhood: Towards a developmental, socioculturally relativistic paradigm. In M. W. Kent & J. R. Rolf (Eds.). *Primary prevention of psychopathology; Vol. 3. Social competence in children* (pp. 253–279). Hanover, NH: University Press of New England.

Laosa, L. M. (1981). Maternal behavior, sociocultural diversity in modes of family interaction. In R. W. Henderson (Ed.), *Parent-child interaction: Research, theory, and prospects.* New York: Academic Press.

Lauderdale, M., Valiunas, A., & Andersen, R. (1980). Race, ethnicity, and child maltreatment: An empirical analysis. *Child Abuse and Neglect, 4,* 163–169.

Leyba, C. (1988). Homicide in Bernalillo County: 1978–1982. In J. F. Kraus, S. B. Sorenson, & P. D. Juarez (Eds.), *Proceedings from the Research Conference on violence and homicide in Hispanic communities* (pp. 101–188). Los Angeles: UCLA Publication Services.

Lockhart, L. L. (1985). A re-examination of the effects of race and social class on the incidence of marital violence: A search for reliable differences. *Journal of Marriage and the Family, 49,* 603–610.

Lockhart, L. L. (1991). Spousal violence: A cross-racial perspective. In R. L. Hampton (Ed.), *Black family violence: Current research and theory* (pp. 85–102). Lexington, MA: Lexington Books.

Lockhart, L. L., & White, B. (1989). Understanding marital violence in the black community. *Journal of Interpersonal Violence, 4*(4), 421–436.

Loya, F., Garcia, P., Sullivan, J. D., Vargas, L. A., Mercy, J., & Allen, N. (1986). Conditional risks among Anglo, Hispanic, Black, and Asian victims in Los Angeles, 1970–1979: Vol. V. Homicide, suicide, and unintentional injuries. *Report of the Secretary's Task Force on Black and Minority Health* (pp. 117–136). Washington, DC: U.S. Department of Health and Human Services.

Lum, J. (1988, March). Battered Asian women. *Rice*, pp. 50–52.

Lynch, E., & Hanson, M. (1992). *Developing cross-cultural competence: A guide for working with young children and their families*. Baltimore, MD: Paul Brookes Publishing.

Marin, G., Sabogal, F., Marin, B. V., Otero-Sabogal, R., & Perez, E. J. (1986). *Cultural values and acculturation among hispanics* (Technical Report No. 3, Hispanic Smoking Cessation Research Project).

Masaki, B. (1992). Shattered myths: Battered women in the A/PI Community. *Focus, 3*, 3.

Mercy, J. A., & Saltzman, L. E. (1989). Fatal violence among spouses in the United States, 1976–85. *American Journal of Public Health, 79*, 595–599.

Messner, S., & Tardiff, K. (1986). Economic inequality and levels of homicide: An analysis of urban neighborhoods. *Criminology, 24*, 297–318.

Moynihan, D. P. (1965). *The negro family: The case for national action*. Washington, DC: U.S. Department of Labor.

Nakagawa, M. (1992, August 14). Domestic violence not a foreign concept in Asian households. *Asian Week*, pp. 1–13.

National Center on Child Abuse and Neglect.(1996). *Child maltreatment 1994: Reports from the States to the National Center on Child Abuse and Neglect*. Washington, DC: U.S. Department of Health and Human Services.

National Center for Health Statistics. (1992). *Vital statistics of the United States, 1989* (Vol. 3, Pl. A). Hyattsville, MD: Author.

National Commission on Children. (1991). *Beyond rhetoric: A new american agenda for children and families* (Final Report). Washington, DC: U.S. Government Printing Office.

National Committee to Prevent Child Abuse. (1995). *Current trends in child abuse reporting and fatalities: The results of the 1994 Annual Fifty State Survey* (Working Paper No. 808). Chicago: National Center on Child Abuse Prevention Research.

National Research Council. (1993). *Understanding child abuse and neglect*. Washington, DC: National Academy Press.

National Research Council.(1994). *Understanding and preventing violence: Vol. 3. Social influences*. Washington, DC: National Academy Press.

National Research Council.(1996). *Understanding violence against women*. Washington, DC: National Academy Press.

Richie, B. E. (1996). *Compelled to crime: The gender entrapment of battered black women*. New York: Routledge.

Rimonte, N.(1989). Domestic violence among Pacific Asians. In Asian Women United of California (Eds.), *Making waves: An anthology of writings by and about Asian American women*. (pp. 327–336). Boston: Beacon Press.

Rodriguez, O. (1988). Hispanics and homicide in New York City. In J. F. Kraus, S. B. Sorenson, & P. D. Juarez (Eds.), *Proceedings from the Research Conference on Violence and Homicide in Hispanic Communities*.(pp. 67–84). Los Angeles: UCLA Publication Services.

Roncek, D. (1981). Dangerous places: Crime and residential environment. *Social Forces, 60*, 74–96.

Saltzman, L. E., Mercy, J. A., Rosenberg, M. L., Elsea, W. R., Napper, G., Sikes, R. K., Waxweiler, R. & the Collaborative Working Group for the Study of Family and Institute Assaults in Atlanta. (1990). Magnitude and patterns of family and intimate assaults in Atlanta, Georgia, 1984. *Violence and Victims, 5*(1), 3–18.

Sampson, R. J. (1983). Structural density and criminal victimization. *Criminology, 21*, 276–293.

Sampson, R. J. (1985). Neighborhood and crime: The structural determinants of personal victimization. *Journal of Research in Crime and Delinquency, 22*, 7–40.

Sampson, R. J. (1986). Neighborhood family structure and the risk of criminal victimization. In J. Byrne & R. Sampson (Eds.), *The social ecology of crime* (pp. 25–46). New York: Springer-Verlag.

Sampson, R. J. (1987). Urban black violence: The effect of male joblessness and family disruption. *American Journal of Sociology, 93*, 348–382.

Sampson, R. J., & Lauritsen, J. L. (1994). Violent victimization and offending: Individual-, situational-, and community-level risk factors. In National Research Council (Ed.), *Understanding and preventing violence: Vol. 3. social influences* pp. (1–95). Washington, DC: National Academy Press.

Schuerman, L., & Kobrin, S. (1986). Community careers in crime. In A. J. Reiss, Jr., & M. Tonry (Eds.), *Communities and crime* (pp. 67–100). Chicago: University of Chicago Press.

Showers, J., & Bandman, R. L. (1986). Scarring for life: Abuse with electric cords. *Child Abuse and Neglect, 10*, 25–31.

Smith, D. R., & Jarjoura, G. R. (1988). Social structure and criminal victimization. *Journal of Research in Crime and Delinquency, 25*, 27–52.

Sorenson, S. B., Stein, J. A., Siegel, J. M., Golding, J. M., & Burnam, M. A. (1987). The prevalence of adult sexual assault: The Los Angeles Epidemiologic Catchment Area project. *American Journal of Epidemiology, 126*, 1154–1164.

Sorenson, S. B., & Telles, C. A. (1991). Self-reports of spousal violence in a Mexican-American and non-Hispanic white population. *Violence and Victims, 6*(1), 3–15.

Sorenson, S. B., Upchurch, D. M., & Shen, H. (1996). Violence and injury in marital arguments. *American Journal of Public Health, 86*, 35–40.

Spearly, J. L., & Lauderdale, M. (1983). Community characteristics and ethnicity in the prediction of child maltreatment rates. *Child Abuse and Neglect, 7*, 91–105.

Staples, R. (1976). Race and family violence: The internal colonialism perspective. In L. Gary & L. Brown (Eds.), *Crime and its impact on the black community*. Washington, DC: Howard University.

Staples, R. & Johnson, L. B. (1993) *Black families at the crossroads: Challenges and prospects*. San Francisco: Jossey-Bass.

Stark, R. (1987). Deviant places: A theory of the ecology of crime. *Criminology, 25*, 893–909.

Straus, M. A., & Gelles, R. J. (1986). Societal change in family violence from 1875 to 1985 as revealed in two national surveys. *Journal of Marriage and the Family, 48*, 465–479.

Straus, M. A., Gelles, R. J., & Steinmetz, S. K. (1980). *Behind closed doors: Violence in the American family*. Garden City, NY: Anchor/Doubleday.

Straus, M. A., & Smith, C. (1990). Violence in Hispanic families in the United States: Incidence and structural interpretations. In M. A. Straus & R. J. Gelles (Eds.),

Committee on Research on Law Enforcement and the Administration of Justice, National Research Council, National Criminal Justice Reference Service.

Thomas, J. (1995a). Dimensions and critical issues of child maltreatment in the African American community: Causation, consequences, and prospects. In *Proceedings of the Institute on Domestic Violence in the African American Community* (pp. 31–52). Washington, DC: U.S. Department of Health and Human Services.

Thomas, J. (1995b). *Violence, conflict, and challenges: A nursing perspective*. American Academy of Nursing Publication.

Urquiza, A., & Wyatt, G. (1994). Culturally relevant violence research with children of color. *American Professional Society on the Abuse of Children (APSAC) Advisor.*

U.S. Advisory Board on Child Abuse and Neglect. (1991). Creating caring communities (Sept.). Washington, DC: U.S. Department of Health and Human Services.

U.S. Advisory Board on Child Abuse and Neglect. (1995). *A Nation's shame: Fatal child abuse and neglect in the United States* (Annual Report). Washington, DC: Department of Health and Human Services, Administration for Children and Families.

U.S. Department of Education, National Center of Educational Statistics. (1992). *The condition of education.* Washington, DC: U.S. Government Printing Office.

U.S. Department of Health and Human Services. (1981). *National study of the incidence and severity of child abuse and neglect: Study findings* (Publication No. OHDS-81003026). Washington, DC: U.S. Government Printing Office.

U.S. Department of Justice. (1986, August). *Preventing domestic violence against women* (Bureau of Justice Statistics Special Report). Washington, DC: U.S. Government Printing Office.

U.S. Department of Justice. (1994, January). *Violence against women* (Bureau of Justice Statistics Special Report No. NCJ-145325). Washington, DC: U.S. Government Printing Office.

U.S. Department of Justice. (1994, July). *Murder in families* (Bureau of Justice Statistics Special Report). Washington, DC: U.S. Government Printing Office.

U.S. Department of Justice. (1994, November). *Violence between intimates* (Bureau of Justice Statistics Special Report No. NCJ-149259). Washington, DC: U.S. Government Printing Office.

U.S. Department of Justice. (1995). *Sourcebook of criminal justice statistics 1994* (Bureau of Justice Statistics). Washington, DC: U.S. Government Printing Office.

U.S. Department of Justice. (1995, August). *Violence against women: Estimates from the redesigned survey* (Bureau of Justice Statistics Special Report No. 154348). Washington, DC: U.S. Government Printing Office.

U.S. Department of Justice, Federal Bureau of Investigation. (1995). *Crime in the U.S. 1994* (Uniform Crime Reports). Washington, DC: U.S. Government Printing Office.

Uzzell, O., & Peebles-Wilkins, W. (1989). Black spouse abuse: A focus on relational factors and intervention strategies. *Western Journal of Black Studies, 13,*10–16.

Valdez, R. B. & Nourjah, R. (1988). Homicide in southern California, 1966–1985: An examination based on vital statistics data. In J. F. Kraus, S. B. Sorenson, & P. D. Juarez (Eds.), *Proceedings from the Research Conference on Violence and Homicide in Hispanic Communities* (pp. 85–100). Los Angeles: UCLA Publication Services.

Williams, C. (1989). *Decision-making for black children in placement in North Carolina* (National Child Welfare Leadership Center, School of Social Work, OJJDP No. 85-JS-CX-K027). Chapel Hill: University of North Carolina.

Williams, K., & Flewelling, R. (1988). The social production of criminal homicide: A comparative study of disaggregated rates in American cities. *American Sociological Review, 53,* 421–431.

Wilson, W. J. (1987). *The truly disadvantaged: The inner city, the underclass, and public policy.* Chicago: University of Chicago Press.

Zahn, M. A. (1988). Homicide in nine American cities: The Hispanic case. In J. F. Kraus, S. B. Sorenson, & P. D. Jarez (Eds.), *Proceedings from the Research Conference on Violence and Homicide in Hispanic Communities* (pp. 13–30). Los Angeles: UCLA Publication Services.

Zellman, G. L. (1992). The impact of case characteristics on child abuse reporting decisions. *Child Abuse and Neglect, 16,* 57–74.

Zimring, F. E., Mukherjee, S. K., & Van Winkle, B. J. (1983). Intimate violence: A study of intersexual homicide in Chicago. *University of Chicago Law Review, 50*(2), 910–930.

The young man of color, in his journey to honorable manhood, will reach a bridge obstructed by older men who have resorted to violence and drug and alcohol abuse as they fight a losing struggle for acceptance by a white-dominated society. The young one must draw upon the traditions of his former society to steer through this confusion and reach solid ground on which he can live as an honorable man with the love and acceptance of his family.
Illustration by Refugio Rodriguez, Santa Maria, CA.

2

El Hombre Noble Buscando Balance: The Noble Man Searching for Balance

Jerry Tello

The ancient teachings, through storytelling, helped to guide, correct, and heal. Through them, the "rites of passage" lessons of "manhood" were conveyed and passed on from one generation to the next. This elder's lesson, which has parallels in many cultures, begins the dialogue and journey toward honorable and balanced manhood.

THE YOUNG MAN AND LIFE'S LESSONS

The viejito, the elder, lived way up on a hill and had been married for many years. His lifelong goal was to have a good relationship with his family, and he was able to do this. Then one day, his wife was called by the other world and left him. But before she left, she said to him, "Remember the promise."

The elder said, "What promise?"

And she answered, "Remember the promise of how we got this house and this land."

And he remembered that the way he got the enormous house and this land was that dueño (the owner) gave it all to them, based on one promise. The promise was that when they were ready to go to that "other place," when they were going to die, they would give it to someone who would continue on with the same valores (values), someone who would live in this house in a way that was harmonious, a way that would make the other happy. The dueño had said, "Remember, before you go, you have to give it to someone who can carry on these valores and make their partner happy."

The viejito remembered, and he realized that his time was getting short. So he called a meeting. He called everybody to the circle, and said, "I'm almost ready to leave and to go to the next world, but first I must keep a promise I made to my wife. I will give this mansion, this huge house and its ten thousand acres, away." (In those days you didn't get houses and you didn't get land unless someone gave them to you.) The viejito continued: "I'm going to give this house and this land to anyone who wants it, as long as he's able to tell me how you can make a harmonious life, how you can make a mujer happy. My life was devoted to my wife, so if you know, as an hombre (man), how to make a mujer happy, then you know how to live in harmony. Now, who among you wants to take the challenge of telling me the four things you have to do, the four values? Who wants to take the challenge of coming back and telling me these four valores? You must do it, however, by the time the sun sets on the seventh day. Do any of you want to take this challenge?"

Four men raised their hands and said that they would take the challenge.

And the viejito said, "There's one thing you should know: Anyone who takes the challenge but doesn't come back with the answers by the time the sun sets on the seventh day, that man will die, and all his generations to come will have disease and will suffer. Now, knowing that, how many of you would still like to take the challenge? Anyone? Remember, this is a huge house, ten thousand acres."

Well, something that happens to men sometimes is that we pretend we're not afraid and that we know everything.

And there was one man like that. "I'll do it!" he said. "Hey! Four values! No problem! I'll get that big house, and the land, and I'll be all set."

So this one man took the challenge. The viejito sent him out and said, "Now, go about the countryside and look for these values among the people, because the values are out there."

Off went the man, walking, and looking, and trying to think of the valores. And he was thinking, maybe one of the valores was to value money. But no, it couldn't be that. Could it be control? No, that couldn't be it. And the harder he thought about it, the harder it was for him to find the values.

As he was walking on this hot day, he became thirsty. He went by the river where there were some children playing in the water. He stopped to get a drink, and seeing the children, he remembered that, being children, these little ones know our spirits, they are honest, they say things we don't want them to say, they do things we don't want them to do, but they're so honest, so clear with us. And the children, seeing this man, knew that he was searching for something, and they asked, "Señor, señor, what's the matter? You look lost—are you looking for something?"

And the man replied, "Ah-h, what do you know? You're just little children, what do you know?"

"Well, what's the matter, sir—what's the matter? You need something?" Then one of the kids whispered, "Hey, he's the one—he's the one! He's the one looking for the valores."

And one of the children spoke up, saying, "You're the one looking for the valores!" Another chided, "Oh, you're going to die if you don't find 'em, huh?"

Because the children know. The children know when we're lost, and they know when something's happening to us, when we're searching. And they're honest—and open—and ready to give us their knowledge, telling us, "We'll tell you! We'll tell you!"

And our usual answer is, "Aw, what do you kids know?"

"Well, we know what makes us happy!" the children said to the man.

"What? What?" asked the man.

"We like cariño (love), we like our moms and dads to hug us and kiss us. We like cariño—we like cariño! We *really* like cariño! It's good! Yeah, that's what we like!"

And the man answered with a sigh, "Well, thank you—thank you."

"Okay! 'Bye, sir—'bye, sir. Hope you find everything you need by the seventh day," the children said, adding "'Cause if not, you're going to die!"

The man continued on his search, and a couple of days passed. He came to some orchards where campesinos (farmworkers) were harvesting fruit, working the land. Seeing the food, and being hungry, he asked one of the men, "Can I have some food?"

"You look a little bit lost and a little bit hungry; of course, you can," the worker said, and gave some fruit to the man. He asked, "Que tiene, señor? (What's the matter, sir?)"

The man replied, "Nothing, nothing. Ah-h-h, you men just work the land, what do you know?"

The worker replied, "No, no, we're close to the land, and we know what's going on. We can feel when something's not right, and you don't seem quite right."

And the man said, "But what do you know?"

Then the worker, talking to one of the others, said, "Ah-h, he's the one, he's the one," and they talked among themselves, saying, "He's the loco (the crazy one), the one who's looking for the valores."

"I'm *not* crazy," the man protested, "but I *am* looking for the values. But what do you know?"

The first worker replied, "Well, we work all day long, every day, and all we want is dignity, just for people to give us valor, to value what we do. We feed the people. We work hard just for one thing: dignity. That's all we ask—all we ask. So that's a value for you."

"Ah, gracias!" the man said. And on he went.

Soon it was the fourth day, then the fifth, and the man was getting a little nervous, starting to think that perhaps he shouldn't have taken on the challenge. He had thought it was going to be easy. As he came to the top of a hill, he saw a little house with a porch, where two viejitos (elders), an old couple, were sitting, drinking coffee, rocking and rocking, and talking to each other.

The man, who was getting tired, wanted a place to sleep, so he went up to the couple and asked, "Have you any place to sleep?"

The old man replied, "We always have room for people passing. Where are you going?" (And the mujer whispered, "He's the one, he's the one!") The viejito, laughing, said, "You're looking for the valores, eh?"

The man answered, "Yes, yes, but I don't know if I'm going to find the four valores soon enough."

The old man replied, "Muy facil, es muy facil (it's very easy)."

"So what do you mean?"

"The old woman replied, "My husband and I, we've been married many years, 60 years, and the most difficult one is him!"

The old man turned to his wife, and said, "Agh, and she likes things in their place, just her way. We fought for years until we learned to respect each other, and we've been together all these years."

So the man stayed overnight with the old couple and realized he had learned a third value: respect. But it was the seventh day, and the sun was in the middle of the sky and now he was back, walking through the village and getting very nervous. As he walked on, he heard a noise somewhere off to the side: "Ps-s-st, p-s-s-t." He looked around, but he saw nothing. Then, he heard the same noise again. "Ps-s-st, p-s-s-t." Suddenly he saw a mujer, saying again, "Ps-s-st, p-s-s-t." He looked. "Ps-s-st, p-s-s-t, come here!" As he drew closer to her, he saw that she was very ugly, with big warts. As he came even closer, he noticed how bad she smelled. Stinking!

The man asked, "Que tiene? (What do you want?)"

The woman said, "So, you're the one looking for the four valores, eh?"

"Yes, but (phew! phew!) what do you know?"

The woman answered, "I've got it for you—I've got the last value!"

"But look at you!" he said with disgust. "You're over here, and you're all stinky and smelly, and what could you know about anything!"

She replied, "Well, I sit here all day long. I see a lot. I know a lot. I see what shouldn't happen. I know. I know the fourth value."

"You don't know anything!"

"Well, it's up to you, señor. What's your choice? If you don't get the value from me, then what? Death. You want to die?"

"No, but you're so ugly, and I . . . "

"Well, it's up to you, señor. Go ahead."

"All right, all right, give me the valor!" he said impatiently.

"No, no, no, no, no!" the woman said solemnly. "You know nothing in this world is free. Life is a circle. I'll give to you, but you give to me."

"But what do you want?"

"If I give you the valor, you have to marry me."

"Marry you!" the man said. "Let's be realistic!"

"Well, it's up to you," she said. "Either you marry me—or you die. Which would you like?"

"Aw, you don't know the value anyway," he muttered.

"Yes, I do."

"Well, what is it?"

"Well, it's very easy." the woman said slowly. "It's palabra. It's giving your word, meaning the value of trust. Trust is such an important thing, and the reason I'm sitting here is because people have broken trust with me. Your palabra, señor. Si no tienes palabra, no tienes nada (if your word isn't trusted, then you have nothing)."

"Agh, that's a stupid value," he replied.

"But you have no choice. It's the last one, eh?"

As the sun began to set, the man ran to the top of the village hill, where sat the viejito, the elder, smiling. "Did you find them?" the old man said. "Did you find them?"

The man answered, "Well, from the children, I learned about love."

"Yes, that's one."

"And from the farmworkers, I learned about dignity."

"Yes, that's the second one."

"From the elders, I learned the value of respect. But I don't know about this last one . . . " The man hesitated.

"Well, what's the last one?"

"Well, it's . . . . , it's trust, and it's about giving your word . . . "

And the viejito says, "Yes, you got it! Where'd you learn about that value?"

"Well, there's this old, ugly woman, sitting on the—"

"No, no, I know about her! But how did you *get* it from her?"

"Well, I promised I'd marry her."

"A-g-h-h-h-h, ho, ho!" the viejito laughed. "So then you will have to marry her, because you can't only have the values, you have to *live* them."

The man looked at the house, and thought, Well, it's a big house; maybe she could live on that side and I'll live on this side, eh?

So the viejito gave them the big house and the land.

And the viejito that night, because his job was done, passed to the next world.

The man and the ugly woman then had a wedding. They invited everyone, and everyone came and celebrated the marriage. After the wedding, the couple went into their house, into the bedroom. There were many bedrooms, but they were in the one room, and the man said, "Well, I'm going to go to another bedroom and sleep, and you can sleep in this bed."

"Yes, okay," replied the woman. "But before you go to sleep, give me a kiss goodnight."

"Do I have to?" he said with revulsion.

"Well, remember the *valores*," she replied, "love, dignity, respect, and . . . come on, kiss me."

"Do I really have to?"

"Yes," she said adamantly.

"Do I have to keep my eyes open?"

"No, you can close your eyes if you want," she said, "just as long as you kiss me."

So, with his eyes closed, the man, thinking that with his eyes closed he would not feel anything, kissed her.

And when he opened his eyes, the woman wasn't ugly anymore. She was beautiful!

And the man said, "Wait a minute! You're not ugly anymore! What happened?"

She replied, "It's because you're not afraid anymore. You were able to get close to what you were afraid of. And when you get close to, and hold, what you fear, it's not ugly anymore. It turns into a lesson about something of beauty. But that's not the end of it."

"What do you mean?" he said.

She replied, "You have a choice."

"What's the choice?"

"Well, I can either be beautiful in the house but ugly when we leave," "or I can be ugly when we're in the house but beautiful when we're outside."

Which would you choose? Ugly when inside the house, beautiful when outside? Or beautiful inside the house, ugly when outside, where all your friends could talk about your ugly wife? If you choose beautiful inside, all your friends will talk about you and wonder how you could marry an ugly woman.

So what did this man do? What did he choose? He had learned something in his life.

Well, what he did is what wise men do, and he said to his wife, "Whatever you want." He gave up his control, He gave up the power, and he allowed the spirit of healing, and of the Creator, to guide him. He gave up trying to dictate.

And with that, she was beautiful inside the house and she was beautiful on the outside, because it didn't matter anymore.

BACKGROUND

Many people, and many Chicano/Latinos as well, do not know that there was a time when there was little violence or fighting among Chicano/Latino people. In fact, many people believe that violence is a part of our core cultural identity.

> Because neither do you understand us, nor do we understand you. And we do not know what it is that you want. You have deprived us of our good order and way of government, and the one with which you have replaced it we do not understand. Now all is confusion and without order and harmony. The Indians of Mexico have given themselves to fighting because you have brought it upon them. . . .

> Those who are not in contact with you do not fight; they live in peace. And if during the time of our "paganism" there were fights and disputes, they were very few. And they were dealt with justly and settled quickly because there used to be no difficulties in finding out which of the parties was right, nor were there any delays and cheating as there are now." (Zurita)

In specific reference to domestic violence, this belief of inbred false perception is so ingrained that some think it is part of being a Chicano/Latino male to beat his wife, a part of his "machismo." It is within this falsehood that the root of the problem lies, the systematic, multigenerational process of internalized oppression.

E. S. Maruse writes that oppression is the "systematic, pervasive, routine mistreatment of individuals on the basis of their membership in a particular group." It is the denial or nonrecognition of the complete humanness of others. Oppression has an order, and the cycle begins with the circulation of lies, misinformation, or half-truths about a people. This misinformation then serves as a justification for their mistreatment. The cycle continues, whereby this misinformation is woven into the fabric of society. The final stage is when the target group believes the lies are attributed to a deficit in their own culture, and they begin internalizing the oppression in actions and behavior against themselves, thus breaking their own true spirit.

This "spirit breaking" came in a variety of direct and indirect measures as a means of the Europeans' attempting to "conquer" the physical, emotional, mental, and spiritual identity of the indigenous Mexican people. This historical genocide resulted in over 50 million people being killed (men, women, and children); thousands of women and children raped; sacred writings, sacred sites, art, and precious belongings destroyed; and the distortion and disharmony of traditional values, customs, ceremonies, and spiritual teachings (Leon-Portilla, 1972). The result of this has been a deep imbalancing wound referred to as intergenerational post-traumatic stress disorder (PTSD) (Duran & Duran, 1995).

At the same time, the wisdom of elders was so profound that the occurrence of these devastating events was actually prophesied by them, long before it came to pass, in the story of "La Llorona" (The Crying Woman) (Leon-Portilla, 1992).

The origin or root of the story is ancient and goes back to before the Europeans invaded Mexico. At this time, there were a number of prophecies, visions, or omens foretelling the arrival of the Spaniards, and one of these omens was that of La Llorona. The people heard a weeping woman, night after night. She passed by in the middle of the night, wailing and crying out in a loud voice, "My children, my children, where will I take you? My children." At other times, she cried, "My children, my children, where are my children?" The indigenous reference for this "crying woman" is Cihuacoatl, an ancient earth goddess, whose principal role was to care for the children. During the time of the European invasion, it has been documented that one of the main preoccupations of the mothers was their fear of "losing" their children. The fear was a literal fear of losing them to death or torture by the invaders, but more importantly, the fear that the children would lose their spirit, their destino, or purpose in life connected to their people. The essence of knowing one's destino was seen as the most significant element of keeping balanced and being well rooted.

In indigenous times, there was much focus and attention devoted to the proper "rooting" or raising of all children, both male and female. An ancient document describing the way the children were taught morals in the past stated that every morning after the children's usual meager breakfast they would be taught:

> How they should live,
>
> How they should respect others,
>
> How they were to dedicate themselves to what was good and righteous,
>
> How they were to avoid evil,
>
> How to flee unrighteousness with strength, and
>
> How to refrain from perversion and greed. (Garibay, n.d.)

The teachings were the same for males and females, and as we see in the next passage, a purity of heart and a sense of spirituality were at the base of these teachings.

Even if he were poor and lowly,

even if his mother and his father

were the poorest of the poor . . .

His lineage was not considered, only his way of life mattered—the purity of his heart,

His good and humane heart . . .

His stout heart . . . .

It was said that he had God in his heart, that he was wise in the things of God. (Torquemada, n.d.)

The above two accounts are directly opposite to the stereotypical view of the "macho" male's self-centeredness. The following account is also contrary to the stereotypical "superior" controlling attitude that is typically considered to be a prerequisite of a traditional Chicano/Latino male:

Not with envy,

not with a twisted heart,

shall you feel superior,

shall you go about boasting.

Rather in goodness shall you make true

your song and your word.

And thus you shall be highly regarded,

and you shall be able to live with the others. (Olmos, n.d.)

In a slightly different way another test describes the good man's just reward:

If you live uprightly,

you shall be held highly for it,

and people will say of you

what is appropriate, what is just. (Olmos, n.d.)

So we see that at the base of the culture were direct teachings to reinforce a sense of respect and interconnectedness founded on spirituality. In addition, contrary to the pervasive "Latin Lover" falsehood and the false stereotype that Latinos didn't talk directly about sexuality, in the following, a father speaks to his son about the importance of sexual moderation and preparation.

Do not throw yourself upon women

Like the dog which throws itself upon food.

Be not like the dog

When he is given food or drink,

Giving yourself up to women before the time comes.

Even though you may long for women,

Hold back, hold back with your heart

Until you are a grown man, strong and robust.

Look at the maguey plant.

If it is opened before it has grown

And its liquid is taken out,

It has no substance.

It does not produce liquid, it is useless.

Before it is opened to withdraw its water,

It should be allowed to grow and attain full size

Then its sweet water is removed all in good time.

This is how you must act:

Before you know woman you must grow and be a complete man.

And then you will be ready for marriage;

You will beget children of good stature,

Healthy, agile, and comely. (Codice Florentino, n.d.)

This passage states, "Before you know woman, you must grow and be a complete man." This reference directs itself to a "rites of passage" that must take place in order that a young man can be ready to enter into a complete relationship with a woman. The passage further states, "And then you will be ready for marriage" or be prepared to make a commitment to another. This aspect of commitment or palabra (word), then, becomes the basis for manhood in the traditional sense; your word, credibility, and essence are based on who and what you represent.

The true essence of what was expected of a man is very clearly articulated in the following passage:

The mature man

Is a heart solid as a rock

Is a wise face

Possessor of a face

Possessor of a heart.

He is able and understanding. (Codice Matritense del Real Palacio)

And finally, in this ancient writing, a father who participates in the raising of children by placing before them a large mirror (his example) is described as compassionate:

The father, root and origin of the lineage of men.

His heart is good, he is careful of things; he is compassionate, he is concerned, he is the foresight, he is support, he protects with his hands.

He raises children, he educates,

He instructs, he admonishes,

He teaches them to live.

He places before them a large mirror,

A mirror pierced on both sides; he is a large torch that does not smoke. (Codice Matritense del la Real Academia, n.d.)

The above reference to a "large torch that does not smoke" speaks again to palabra, or word, that is honest and consistent.

These last two accounts clearly articulate the basis of what the traditional elders described as a "macho" in the true sense of palabra, or word.

"Possessor of a face"—cara.

"Possessor of a heart"—corazon.

So complex are these instructions that 14 volumes are devoted to these teachings alone in the Florentine Codex, an ancient indigenous document. The development of one's character, identity, or root essence was paramount to the ancients because they understood that if the root of the tree was not well grounded, then the tree would be weak and vulnerable to the winds. This identity root, based on the dual concepts of cara y corazon, is reflected in the four main values.

The cara reveals the significance of a man knowing his destino (purpose in life)—his role within the family and community—and a commitment to the interdependent functioning of the family. The two values that form the basis of cara are dignidad (dignity) and respeto (respect).

In balancing this duality, the corazon reveals the need for compassion and trust, a spiritual harmony and a sense of understanding and consideration for others. The two values that form the basis of corazon are confianza (interconnected bonding) and carino (love, acceptance).

It is with this knowledge that the "true" definition of macho, based on the indigenous elders' teachings, can be understood:

Dignified

A Protector

Responsible

Nurturing

Spritual

Faithful

Respectful

Friendly

Caring

Sensitive

Trustworthy. (Codice Matritense del la Real Academia, n.d.)

So the teachings are still there, even though many do not know they exist. If you destroy the semblance of a people's authentic self, you destroy their spirit. Thus, we truly begin to understand the tremendous trauma that was perpetrated and the disequilibrium that was manifested—so profound in nature that we feel it still, even today. This tremendous historical, multigenerational distortion of our way of life impacted us to the degree that we, as a people, still are attempting to rebalance from the over 50 million deaths, rapes, and severe abuses that were perpetrated on our people. The total disequilibriating impact of destroying a harmonious, interdependent identity has now resulted in some of us hurting, killing, and violating our own as a way of life. This brings extreme sadness and pain to so many. And if that were not enough, these oppressive forces have been successful in having many believe that these negative, spirit-destroying acts of violence against women, the center of our people, are part of our cultural identity, a spirit-destroying lie that evokes deep hopelessness.

The end result of this belief is shame, resulting finally in a total psychospiritual amnesia of one's true spirit. This long-term spirit-breaking process continues to have a devastating effect on Chicano/Latinos as a whole, and with reference to domestic violence, we see the harmful effects daily. Fortunately, the spirit of ancients is very strong and thus we, as a people, have been able to maintain a semblance of our destino whereby the mujer (woman) and mother is still held with much respect and honor by many as an ideal, and in practice as well. This is not to say that the multigenerational oppression has not had its effect. Furthermore, I believe that unless we re-root the true essence of the ancient teachings quickly, we may lose our total rooted spirit.

We find in approaching this issue of "El Hombre Noble Buscando Balance" (The Noble Man Searching for Balance) that we have men at different points on the journey.

As part of this journey, there is a symbol of a "bridge crossing" rite of passage phase in every young person's life that is seen as critical in defining that person's development. The following is the way "The Bridge Story" came to me in a dream:

It was said that one of the greatest gifts of the dual forces coming together was that of creation—and so it was from woman and man in connection and commitment to each other and the community that the young ones were gifted to the world. It was man (father) who had as his role the raising and guiding of the children, and woman (mother) had as her role the nurturing and caring for the children, as did all the community. But after a time, when the crying woman's (La Llorona) prophecy had come true and the people were struggling, there was a young girl whose time it was to approach the bridge. Since woman/mother gave life, she was given the privilege of guiding her children to the bridge. So it was that this mother took her daughter to the woman's bridge (as there are two bridges), and she found a group of women standing in a circle at the foot of the bridge, talking and sharing. This was expected, as young girls are raised to share and care for each other, and to gather in circles.

The mother approached the women and asked them to help guide her daughter across the woman's bridge. The women readily accepted and encircled the young girl for the journey. A few days later, it was time for another to take her son to the man's bridge. As she approached the man's bridge, she looked but could find no one at the foot of the bridge. Needing someone to accompany her son, she continued to look and saw a group of men halfway across the bridge. They were arguing, drinking, and fighting with each other. She called out to them and asked them to accompany her son across the bridge. The men looked at each other in confusion, wondering to whom she was talking. Again, the mother called out to the men for assistance, and once again, they were dismayed. As boys, they had been raised to take care only of themselves and not to care for and nurture others. The mother called out again, asking if they would come and accompany her son across the bridge.

In the midst of this shouting, one man spoke up and said, "How do you expect us to take a young boy across the bridge when some of us grown men haven't even been across ourselves?"

"Then what should I do with my son?" asked the mother.

"Just leave him here with us," replied the man. So the mother left her son in the midst of the men who, themselves, were struggling.

As she went back to the village, very concerned, the other women noticed her worry and asked her, "Why?" She replied, "All the men I saw were arguing, fighting, drinking, lying, and cheating." She then turned to her young daughter and said, "Be careful with the men; they can't be trusted."

As she gave this advice to her daughter, her younger son also heard and learned to distrust men and, more importantly, to distrust himself.

Another mother approached the bridge with her son and was able to look through the men halfway across the bridge and see her husband, who had barely reached the other side. As she called out to him to come get his son, he said, "But I barely made it here myself! I just recently stopped drinking and going out. I'm afraid if I go past those men, I may get caught again because the pain that drew me to the middle is still present. I'm sorry; I can't."

There are many good men, but they hide themselves in their work, or in sports, or inside themselves. They spend very little time with their children, wives, or families, because to do this would open their hearts not only to love but also to their pain-ridden past. They may distance themselves emotionally from those they love most, only to someday explode unexpectedly.

There are many Chicano/Latino men, however, who have made it across the bridge, while maintaining their identity, values, traditions, and spirituality, but the oppressive society does not acknowledge or recognize them. These are not the men whom we generally see in domestic violence, alcohol, or drug treatment programs, because they are busy being good grandfathers, fathers, husbands, sons, brothers, and friends to their family and community.

"The Bridge Story" begins to explain the complexity of the issues as we attempt to understand the impact of multigenerational oppression in reference to working with Chicano/Latino men and domestic violence. What we find is that this sociohistorical trauma has affected them to different degrees whereby they fall at different places on what I have termed the Psychocultural Digressionary Scale. There are five stages to this process.

1. PSYCHOCULTURAL CONFUSION

This is a state in which the multigenerational effects of oppression confuse the people to the degree that their internal sense of spiritual identity still gives them signals that their aggressive, forceful ways are inappropriate to their true cultural base. Although they "know" that their aggression is culturally inappropriate, they are confused by society's message of male dominance, compounded by the lack of "true" knowledge in reference to their own culturally balanced sense of being un noble hombre (a noble male).

2. INTERNALIZED ANGER

This often occurs as the traditional ceremonies and traditions of healing, cleansing, and rebalancing have been invalidated by society as being not necessary. This results in confusion about the changing values, the changing roles for men and women, along with continued invalidation by an oppressive society, which causes men to feel insecure and to begin questioning their destino (purpose in life). With the traditional extended support and healing systems (compadres, temezcallis, hombres circles) no longer in place, their inadequate feelings are internalized and manifested in several ways:

Generalized apathy (unmotivated)
Generalized fear (rigid)
Hypersensitivity (reactive, moody).

3. INTERNALIZED OPPRESSION (HATE)

At this point in the digressionary process, men begin to believe that the oppression and mistreatment by society is deserved and is due to an inadequacy in the Chicano/Latino culture. Many people at this stage falsely believe that male dominance, sexism, and domestic violence are a part of the Chicano/Latino identity, thus validating their abusive behavior. Unconsciously, they begin integrating many oppressive processes: violence, infidelity, and negative coping methods (drugs, alcohol, fleeing) as a maladaptive way of attempting to survive and maintain their "value." To justify their behavior, they blame the victims. People at this stage encircle themselves with others who reinforce their behavior.

Distrust in self and others (controlling, jealous)
Anger turned outward (hostility, acting out)
Self harm (drugs, alcohol, violence).

4. Dissociative Patterns of Behavior (Self-hate)

At this stage, the oppression has been internalized so deeply that the expectations of male behaviors and treatment of women are based on the false, imbalanced sense of continuing the cycle. The cultural shame is so pervasive that there is a general mistrust, dislike, and avoidance of Chicano/Latino men. Gang violence, men fighting each other, and women stating, "I'll never marry a Chicano/Latino man," are symptoms. Individual day-to-day survival becomes the focus, and a systematic process of separating oneself from one's actions, and the harm caused by them, is common. People at this stage have trouble differentiating between self-sabotaging behavior and life-enhancing, culturally appropriate behavior.

Anger turned inward (self hate)
Established alternative rules (survival)
Fatalism (lack of hope).

5. Psychospiritual Amnesia (Rage)

At this point, men have no recollection or memory of true Chicano/Latino cultural authenticity. They believe their negative adaptive behaviors are part of the cultural expectations. This occurs many times when children are born into a family that is functioning at stage 3, 4, or 5. No one has taught the children the true cultural expectations of being un hombre noble, of being a persona con palabra (a person with credibility). Therefore, the children grow up with a false sense of who they are and what they should be. Rage-based, destructive behavior is a symptom of full-blown psychospiritual amnesia.

What makes the healing and rebalancing process more difficult and complex are the present-day oppressive processes that continue to torment the Chicano/Latino people. With the intensified immigrant bashing and English-only movements in full force, it makes it difficult to focus on the problem behavior without addressing the ongoing societal trauma. Any attempts to re-root the imbalanced, pain-ridden men in their true manhood identity are often seen by mainstream practitioners as not directly dealing with their behavior. In addition, the so-called leaders in the field of domestic violence, those who work with batterers, control the definition of what is acceptable theory, practice, and intervention, thus directly and indirectly continuing the oppression that has been perpetrated on the Chicano/Latino community for generations.

With this in mind, we see how it becomes necessary to not only address the imbalanced, violent behavior that is a symptom of a deeper, self-denigrating, spiritual identity violation, but to address it in the context of the total past and present-day social-historical oppression. More importantly, we must recognize that the effects of the oppressive trauma have been not only on the so-called abuser but on the family and community as well. This, therefore, necessitates encircling the entire healing process with a philosophy that is consistent with and indigenous to the identity ceremonies, traditions, and principles of the Chicano/Latino people themselves.

LA CULTURA CURA / THE HEALING TREE PHILOSOPHY

Families, communities, and societies since the beginning of time have had to confront issues that appeared to threaten the very essence of their purpose. Even in those times when there seemed to be no hope for revitalization, a way has shown itself.

Traditionally, in all communities, there was a sacred tree where individuals, families, and the community as a whole would gather. That tree, the symbolic focal point, rod of life, or spiritual altar, in more recent times is seen as a church, synagogue, community center, or the home of the community healer/leader. Where this "place of the tree" truly served its community purpose, it became the reference point from which one gained clarity of purpose, healing, and strength. It then was the role of each person and family to take the spirit of this "tree" into their homes and instill its meaning into the members of their family. It is for this reason that many families have a spiritual altar in a special place in their homes.

At the same time, it was evident to all that the "weak wind," the "coyote spirit," or negative influences of the world were a constant threat to the harmony and balance of the individual, the family, and the community. It was for this reason that families and communities began to understand that in order to survive and grow, they, like the tree, must be re-rooted in positive principles.

People—men, women, elders—gathered in circles as a manner of honoring and keeping in harmony with those principles. In these circles, and through positive ceremonies, traditions, and customs, the principles were taught, reinforced, and strengthened. Therefore, the principles provided the way for the individual, the family, and the community to carry out their larger purpose in life, and the ceremonies and traditions ensured that they were taught and maintained.

Various tribes, subgroups of Chicano/Latino people, have developed interpretations of the principles and ceremonies based on the particular "way" of their rooted ethnic spirit. Although ceremonial expression of these rituals and principles is different, depending on the particular region, it is found that ethnic-centered people of all roots have gathered, and continue to gather, in circles (men, women, family/community) to strengthen, rebalance, and maintain harmony.

The healing tree philosophy (Codice Matritense del Real Palacio, n.d.) is used to symbolically emphasize the need for a positive, centering base of principles that assist Chicano/Latino males to maintain their balance, and grow. It is also used to illustrate the various elements that affect an individual and family/community, positively or negatively, in this process.

1. *Purpose/Destino: Based on Individual, Family/Community Dignity (Dignidad)*

A basic premise of individual, family/community dignity acknowledges that within the ancestral wisdom of a people are the teachings and medicine necessary for growth and healing. The teachings or healing elements inevitably come from the people themselves. Therefore, in order for healing, or rebalance, to be successful, and although the initial incentive may come from an outside person, the ongoing motivation for individual, family/community growth and rebalancing must come from within the circle of those who desire or need growth and change.

2. *Responsibility: Based on Respect (Respeto) for Family/Community Vision*

Individuals must have a vision that reflects the potential of their true self in reference to their family/community. If a person has only a negative view of himself and his culture, then he has no avenue for growth or development.

A person's primary ethnicity is the root of the vision. It is necessary for the person to dream, reflect, and rediscover the life-enhancing values and gifts of his own indigenous culture. It is necessary to know and understand his history in order to understand the process that created his present situation. By this process, and with the proper guidance, a person will be able to separate pain and dysfunction from the strength of its culture. As part of their indigenous heritage, all people have ceremonies and rituals for clarifying and rediscovering their vision of growth. These ceremonies and rituals must be integrated and practiced in a balanced, consistent manner.

3. *Interdependence: Based on Individual,*
   Family/Community Trust (Confianza)

The strengthening of a community, and the families within it, directly enhances the development and healing of its individuals. As individuals heal and grow, they reintegrate with the positive vision of the community. Families/communities, and the individuals within them, must develop interdependently. If one is missing, then disharmonious growth occurs, which leads to false hope and development. It is essential to know the difference between codependence, individualism, and indigenous cultural interdependence.

4. *Development: Circular Learning Based on Love (Cariño) for Life*

A love for life is the basis of a circular learning process. As times change, people must learn "new" ways (based on ancient teachings) to live in the world as individuals, families, and communities. There must be pride in one's root ethnicity and respect for those of another root. The new ways must be both life-preserving and life-enhancing. In addition, organizations, institutions, and dominant societal communities must learn to live in new ways.

5. *Enthusiasm: Living Life with a Sense of Spirit (Espíritu)*

Living life with a sense of spirit (spirituality) allows an individual, family/community to approach life with an element of enthusiasm (ganas). Instilling or reinstilling that sense of spirituality in an individual, family/community allows one to deal with the difficult, and sometimes overwhelming, day-to-day pressures with a sense of hope and "greater spirit."

With the healing tree as the philosophy for reframing and addressing this issue of manhood and violence, the previous principles are used as a basis for re-rooting and recentering the behavior and spirit of the men. The true indigenous expectation of Chicano/Latino men as hombres nobles (noble men) begins to redefine the values and behaviors that are appropriate and acceptable. A traditional process of an extended kinship network, or circulo de hombres, a healing, rebalancing, and accountability process is reintroduced and initiated in these men's lives in order that, collectively, they can complete their journey across the bridge. In addition, establishing this circle of support (compadres) gives them a place to heal from the wounds of oppression and effectively confront the day-to-day stressors as hombres nobles.

CIRCULO DE HOMBRES (CIRCLE OF MEN): HEALING

One of the main elements of approaching an issue, such as domestic violence, is how you define it. In Western psychotherapeutic approaches to this issue, it continues to be standard to use a box-oriented framework to categorize, intervene, and evaluate progress. On the other hand, the traditional indigenous way is to look at things not in terms of good or bad, victim or perpetrator, but in terms of balance, of harmony, of the circular nature of life. That circular nature stresses an important point: If you share balance and harmony, they come back to you; if not, you must deal with what you have given. With the circular nature in mind, and based on the previous emphasis on healing from oppression and colonization, we acknowledge and recognize that most Chicano/Latino men in treatment are carrying not only their own unresolved baggage but that of their fathers, grandfathers, etc. This acknowledgment brings to light the choice for us, as men: to be a noble man and attempt to heal and balance the pain, or irresponsibly give the baggage to the next generation, thus abdicating our manhood expectation. In addition, based on the healing tree philosophy, we acknowledge that we all come to the circle with regalos (gifts) and cargas (baggage) and lessons to teach each other. This aspect of nosotros (all of us) having gifts and baggage and lessons to teach puts men in the role of being accountable but without reoppressing them with categories and labels.

THE FOUR DIRECTIONS

The intervention process itself utilizes the traditional four dimensions of life: physical, emotional, mental, and spiritual, incorporated within a four-phase framework.

- Conocimiento: In this phase, the focus is the acknowledgment of who the person is and what he brings to the circle. What is his palabra, meaning who and what does he represent? This is the core element in building confianza (trust).
- Entendimiento: The aspect of understanding, or reunderstanding, the journey of each person in the circle is the emphasis here. The aspects of history, oppression, and uncovering the authentic hombre noble are the focuses.
- Integration: The application of being able to live and maintain balance and harmony, in spite of the "coyote's" presence, is the focus.

The "coyote spirit" is used as the trickster elements in one's life that attempt to draw the person off-balance.

- Movimiento: This final phase focuses on the ongoing reestablishment of traditions and customs that help maintain the balance. The interconnected lifelong responsibility of being an example and a compadre to other men is emphasized.

As seen in a circle, there is no beginning, no end. This reinforces the idea that the lessons of life will always be present and that one has the choice of how he can approach these lessons and handle them in life.

What is occurring is the regrounding and the establishment of destino (positive purpose) in the lives of men, with the interconnected checks and balances of positive traditions and customs. The circulo becomes the extended kinship network that supports but also makes all members accountable. The degree of healing and cleansing depends on a multitude of factors, but with the spirit reintroduced in their lives, men are given a viable option to continue to live their lives based on more than just day-to-day survival.

As one heals and grows, we all heal and grow, thus shedding a wounded layer of oppression that will make the lives of future generations much happier and more harmonious.

Un Hombre Noble / A Noble Man . . .

- Es un hombre que cumple con su palabra (Is a man of his word).
- Debe de tener un sentido de responsabilidad para su propio bienestar y para otros en su circulo (Should have a sense of responsibility for his own well-being and that of others in his circle).
- Rechaza cualquier forma de abuso: fisico, emocional, mental, u espiritual a si mismo o a otras personas (Rejects any form of abuse: physical, emotional, mental, or spiritual, to himself or others).
- Debe de tener tiempo para refleccionar, rezar y incluir la ceremonia en su vida (Should take time to reflect, pray, and include ceremony in his life).
- Debe de ser sensible y comprensivo (Should be sensitive and understanding).
- Debe de ser como un espejo, reflejando apoyo y claridad de uno a otro (Should be like a mirror, reflecting support and clarity to one another).
- Vive estos valores honradamente y con amor (Lives these values honestly, and with love).

REFERENCES

Codice Florentino, Book VI, fol. 97, r., and Sahagun, Historia, I, 554. (n.d.)
Codice Matritense del Real Palacio, VI, fol. 215. (n.d.)
Codice Matritense del la Real Academia, VIII 118, V. (n.d.)
Garibay, (tr.), "Huehuetlatolli, Documento A," loc. cit., 97/ (n.d.)
Leon-Portilla, M. (1972). *Los antigua Mexicanos*. Mexico: Fondo de Cultura Economico.
Leon-Portilla, M. (1972). *The broken spears: The Aztec account of the conquest of Mexico*.
Maruse, S. S. (n.d.)
Olmos, Mss en Nahuatl, fol. 112, r. (n.d.)
Olmos, Mss en Nahuatl, fol. 188, r. (n.d.)
Torquemada, op. cit., I, 1988. (n.d.)
Zurita, Breve y Sumaria Relacion. . ., in Icazbalceta (ed.), Nueva Coleccion de Doc-
    umentos para la Historia de Mexico, III. (n.d.)

The Healing Tree represents a centering base of principles that assists the growth of the individual and the community. See the "Healing Tree Philosophy," p. 47. *Illustration by Refugio Rodriguez, Santa Maria, CA.*

3

Clinical Treatment of Latino Domestic Violence Offenders

Ricardo Carrillo and Rolando Goubaud-Reyna

El Respeto al Derecho Ajeno, es la conservacion de la Paz.
To Respect Others Rights is the preservation of Peace.

—Bentito Juarez

Evaluation and treatment models for male batterers have developed in quantity and sophistication over the past 15 years (Gondolf, 1988). These programs purport a variety of methods, from short-term treatment (Dutton, 1988) to long-term reeducation of sexist attitudes (Sinclair, 1990), intensive psychotherapy, and anger management (AMEND, 1990). Treatment approaches, with their foundations based in theory, mirror current psychological approaches to professional practice. Psychoeducational formats popular with court-mandated programs (Dutton, 1988), feminist programs advocating restructuring of sexist attitudes toward women (Sinclair, 1990), comprehensive and thorough long-term psychotherapy models, and individual, group, and, when appropriate, marital family therapy (Flores-Ortiz, Esteban, & Carrillo, 1994) are some examples of eclectic approaches to the treatment of the male offender of domestic violence. These strategies are by no means exhaustive of the current methods utilized by practitioners (Caesar & Hamberger, 1989; Gondolf, 1988).

Empirical research on male batterers has been limited to small samples (Saunders, 1979), theoretical explanations of the etiology of violent behavior (Strauss & Gelles, 1990), and comparisons of personality measures of offenders pre- and posttreatment (Dutton, 1989). Results of these studies are inconclusive, partially from lack of empirical research on program effectiveness with male batterers. Crosscultural studies in comparison are limited (Brice-Baker, 1994; Cervantes & Cervantes, 1993; Neff, Holamon & Schluter, 1995; Sorenson & Telles, 1987).

A paucity of research and effective treatment models for treating Latino male offenders exists in the literature (Carrillo, 1985; Cervantes & Cervantes, et al, 1993). This chapter is a clinical treatment approach that attempts to fill the void for the practitioner committed to assisting Latino men in stopping their violence against family members.

Contemporary services for family violence are fragmented in their focus. Services are available for "victims, offenders," and children suffering from the effects of domestic violence. The end result appears to have essentially taken the "family" out of family violence. Within the current treatment programs, each individual family member is treated out of the context of the family system, many times at odds with each other. Each separate population has its own issues and advocates. The treatment itself retraumatizes the family, first, by catching family members in the vicious cycle of violence, and second, by developing fragmented treatment systems.

Currently, family systems protocols are being explored as methods for the treatment of violent families (Crillio & DeBlasio, 1992; Goldner, Walter, Penn, & Wienberg, 1992). With limited validation in the field of domestic violence treatment, we propose an interconnected approach, particularly with Latino offenders and their families. Emphasizing individual and family rebalancing, victims' safety, cessation of the batterers' violence, and family reintegration when and if appropriate in the later stages of treatment is the total focus. The literature indicates that family systems approaches for Latino families can be extremely beneficial (Cervantes & Cervantes, 1993). A comprehensive systemic approach for working with violent Latino families, including a gradual progression from careful diagnostics to multiple generational family therapy, appears promising. A holistic approach, which attempts to replace the fragmentation of the family's traumatic violent experiences (social, historical oppression) with hope and healing (cultural rerooting), is the basic theoretical viewpoint of this treatment protocol.

The proposed treatment protocol has four phases; each has been described conceptually by Tello (1992) as part of the Family Healing Tree. Phase 1 is Diagnostic/conocimiento; phase 2 is the Understanding or psychoeducation/entendimiento; phase 3 is Internal movement or process psychotherapy/integracion; and phase 4 is Integrated movement or completion of the healing circle/movimiento, when the client becomes an elder/advocate for new clients entering therapy. The following sections will describe the family healing tree philosophy as it is applied to the treatment of violent Latino families.

LA CULTURA CURA: THE HEALING TREE PHILOSOPHY

Tello describes the healing tree in this fashion:

> Since the beginning of time, people have gathered in circles as a matter of honoring and keeping in harmony with the natural rhythm and movement of life. It was these ceremonial circles that strengthened and kept the people focused to the larger purposes in life. Various tribes or groups of people have developed traditions and customs that are built on the particular style of the rooted ethnic spirit of their people. Although the ceremonial expression of these rituals is different depending on the particular group of people, it is found that ethnic-centered people of all roots have gathered and continue to gather in circles for . . . rite of passage and times of pain and distress. There would be times when tragedy, famine, illness would befall a community and at these times people would gather to reflect, pray, discuss, and attempt to understand the greater lesson in order that they could appropriately, as a community, deal with the situation.
>
> The concepts of cara y corazon (face and heart) are also directly related to the traditional indigenous concept of la educacion (character development), which for Latino families is a fundamental principle for appropriate living. The cara noble (noble face) is reflective of the values of dignity and respect. The corazon firme (firm heart) mirrors the values of confianza (trustworthiness; interdependent, intuitive bonding) and carino (love and acceptance). A person who is bien educado (has a good character) has a balanced sense of cara y corazon. . . . In a pain-ridden, substance-dependent, or violent home, it is these . . . values that are severely traumatized and ultimately cast parents who have come from these homes as high risk for maintaining pain-filled legacies.
>
> Traditionally in all communities there was a sacred tree where families and the community would gather. This tree became the symbolic focal point, rod of life, or spiritual altar that was the reference point for gaining clarity, healing, and strength. It was very clear that in order for a community to survive and grow it must be rooted in strong principle. Therefore, the principles (dignidad, respeto, confianza, and carino) provide the way for the community. (Tello, 1992, p. 13)

The treatment process must mirror the values of the healing tree. The therapist must reflect the cara y corazon expected of the clients in order to model for them how to walk in balance.

PHASE 1: DIAGNOSTIC/CONOCIMIENTO

Phase 1 focuses on connecting with and gaining knowledge of the gifts and baggage of the person. It also specifically concentrates on the assessment of lethality, the thorough diagnostic evaluation of the cycle of violence, intergenerational as well as episodic assessment of mental illness, neuropsychological impairment, and the amenability for treatment. Research in the area of lethality in domestic violence has recently increased (Browne, 1986; Walker, 1984). Browne's (1986) research found several variables to be significant with battered women who had murdered their abusive spouses. The variables included an increase in the severity and frequency of the violence, higher indices of injuries, use of alcohol and drugs, prior criminal justice involvement on the part of the batterer, use of weapons and/or threats of weapons use, and a paralyzing psychological intrusion of their "space." Threats of suicide and homicide were frequent in the lethal cases of domestic violence. In addition, mental illness and a history of neurological impairment may contribute to an increase in the likelihood of the cycle of violence reaching lethal proportions. An assessment of lethality is essential, but the assessment of psychospiritual strengths are also important.

Referrals made to our treatment program are routinely assessed for mental illness, neuropsychological impairment, and level of denial. If the offender is not mentally ill, neurologically impaired, developmentally disabled, then the question of amenability for treatment rests on the willingness to accept responsibility for stopping the violence (giving his word "palabra") . Dual problem areas such as alcoholism and substance abuse need to be treated simultaneously with the domestic violence program.

> Manuel was referred to treatment by the probation department. He spoke primarily Spanish, but could understand English as well. He migrated from Guatemala and has been in the United States for 6 years. He is attractive and charming, and presents a convincing scenario that he had accidentally "shoved" his wife. Upon specific questioning and challenging by the group leader and other men in the group, he reveals that in fact he had severely battered his partner, pushing her, pinning her to the ground, slapping her with an open hand, and choking her. Manuel is then asked if he is willing to be un hombre de palabra, accountable for his violence, and if he is willing to stop the violence. At the same time, Manuel is asked to account for his history of being violent to his partner, children, and previous partners. Manuel is called to examine his history of being victimized as well. If Manuel is ready to account for his violence and victimization toward his partner and family, he was asked to so acknowledge. Manuel is ready. The men in the group agree to support him in the group process (Sinclair, 1990).

The purpose of any initial psychotherapy process or healing journey is to understand who the man is. What are his strengths (gifts/regalos)? What are his limitations (baggage/cargas)? Is he amenable and willing to face his shame/verguenza for having battered his partner/companera and/or his children? Is he willing to participate in the ceremony/ceremonia of psychotherapy? Is he suffering from a major mental disorder, neuropsychological condition, active chemical-dependent behavior? Can he work within the limited structure of an outpatient setting? Or is his violence so that he requires more structure than an outpatient setting?

The primary treatment expectations of the program are clearly defined in a contract, which explains the program and the client's obligations for successful completion—attendance, payment of fees, confidentiality, maintenance of sobriety, and a willingness to stop the violence—along with an acknowledgment that the program will maintain contact with the offender's partner.

The initial phase also focuses on the social learning principles and the effects of colonialization. The principles helping the offenders to take responsibility for their violence.

In summary, phase 1 is the assessment of the individual, his family's intergenerational history, and his amenability to participate in treatment.

PHASE 2: UNDERSTANDING OR PSYCHOEDUCATION/ENTENDIMIENTO

The exploration of the men's values/valores is the focus of this phase. The men examine the meanings of respect/respeto, dignity/dignidad, nurture/carino, trust/confianza, anger/coraje vs. rage and shame/verguenza because their violent behavior breaks down such values, not only at the intrapersonal level, but at the intrafamilial level. Thus, they can understand how their violence destroys the trust/confianza that once existed in the family. Without trust/confianza, there is no respect/respeto. Without these, the dignity and love die. Since these men often feel that love, and respect are "services" women and children ought to provide, they say they feel "forced" to demand such "services" by violent means. If so, what did these values mean to them as children, and how were they frozen/conjelados as they grew up developmentally? The migration from their home countries and the discrimination, marginalization, and racist stereotyping have contributed to their misunderstanding of the original meaning of these values (Flores-Ortiz, Esteban, & Carrillo 1994). In addition, three separate periods of colonization have contributed to their misrepresentation of these original values (Griswold-Del Castillo, 1984). Cognitive restructuring prepares them for healthier definitions of these values/valores and the subsequent appropriate behavioral responses.

Understanding the personal history of violence and its consequences is the emphasis of this phase. The applied psychological principles of cognitive behavioral training for the cessation of domestic violence (Sonkin, Martin, & Walker, 1985), the reeducation of sexist patriarchal attitudes (Sinclair, 1995), and the influence of colonialization are the parameters of treatment for this phase (Griswold-Del Castillo, 1984; Freire, 1972). Psychoeducational approaches such as assertiveness training and anger management have proven effective in treating a variety of symptomatic behaviors, including anxiety, depression, and chemical dependency (Beck, 1976; Meichenbaum, 1977). These approaches seem to prepare Latino offenders to learn how to be responsible for their physiological responses to arousal, their cognitions, and their affective responses, ultimately leading to an awareness of a repertoire of behaviors. Prior to this psychoeducational experience, Latino men, like other batterers, appear to be unaware of the relationship of stimulation and emotional and cognitive responses to their behavior. This approach prepares them for the development of effective behavioral management.

Domestic violence has been defined as any form of physical, mental, emotional, and sexual abuse by an intimate toward another for the exclusive purpose of dominating and controlling the partner (Pence & Paymar, 1993; Sonkin & Durphy, 1989). Inherent in the abuse of the family is the dimension of spiritual violence. The violation of the psychological space, thoughts, feelings, and beliefs of a family member is considered spiritual violence. Violence hurts the heart/spirit of the family members involved (Mandanes, 1990; Thin Elk, personal communication, February 12, 1992). Latino men, although a heterogeneous lot, share cultural beliefs regarding spirituality. In fact, violent offenders commonly find solace and repentance in God or the church of choice. However, the violation of a family's spiritual character is the responsibility of the offender. Latino men are traditionally socialized to protect their families, and the paradox is that after several periods of colonialization (Griswold-Del Castillo, 1984), they have become the oppressor in the home (Freire, 1972). It appears to be necessary to develop an awareness of the events of colonial history in order to have the men in treatment understand that their behavior has been learned and socialized. It is understandable that Native and Mestizo men have been indoctrinated to believe that they are inferior and incapable of providing or protecting their families. It is our premise that domestic violence in the Latino male population has its roots in European colonialization.

Effective interventions with Latino offenders require bilingual and bicultural staff. It is imperative that the staff be trained in domestic violence issues as well as cultural sensitivities with the Latino population they service. The Latino population in the Southwestern region of the United States includes Mexican immigrants, Central/South American immigrants, Caribbean migrants, and bilingual/bicultural Hispanos from Colorado, New Mexico, and Texas. The heterogeneity of these populations requires the treatment program to be well versed in language, colloquialism, cultural beliefs, values, customs, rituals, and ceremonies particular to each cultural group.

Another example is the Eastern Seaboard. This area has immigrants from the Caribbean, Puerto Rico, Cuba, the Dominican Republic, and Central and South America. Therefore, any treatment program must take into account the cultural nuances of the country of origin. Culturally relevant staffing patterns and respectful approaches to dealing with the client population are imperative for maintaining clients in treatment. It is also imperative that the worldview of the population being served be respected.

Classic differences in worldview values between mainstream American/European and Latino populations include:

individualism	vs.	group
competition	vs.	cooperation
materialism	vs.	spirituality
content (product)	vs.	process (relatedness)
patriarchy	vs.	egalitarianism

These need to be taken into consideration when treating this population.

PATRIARCHY

Although Latino populations are heterogeneous, patriarchy is a shared belief among many Latino immigrants, especially among domestic violence offenders (Flores-Ortiz, et al. 1994; Mirandé & Enriques, 1979). Social learning and cognitive behavioral theories postulate that cognitions, beliefs, and behaviors are learned overtly and covertly by modeling and reinforcement contingencies. Patriarchal notions among Latino men vary with age, class, and socioeconomic status. However, the offender population shares the belief that women are subservient to men. The women's position in the family is to serve the men.

Objectification, or the "thingafying" of women (Internalized oppression) becomes a reasonable belief (Sinclair, 1990). The classic stereotype of the Latino family marital power structure is described by Bernal, Flore-Ortiz, &

Rodriguez-Draguin (1986), quoting Diaz-Guerrero, Lichtszajn, & Reyes (1979):

> The hierarchical organization of the family is clear. The father is the head of the house, he is the indisputable authority and deserves respect and obedience. He is in charge of financial matters, he is the fountain of economic support and makes all of the family investments . . . . The woman is considered, traditionally, the fountain of emotional support for the family. She is responsible for the raising of the children, and the care of the home. In return for devotion and warmth, she is the object of adoration and protection. (p. 3)

What is important to understand is that this is the imbalanced result of colonialization.

According to Diaz-Guerrero et al. (1979), this distinction of the masculine and feminine roles is founded in the belief of the biological superiority of the male. Support for these types of beliefs can be found in messages proscribed in cultural proverbs (dichos) used for teaching appropriate conduct to children. The following proverbs have a direct relationship to the accepted worldview of male superiority.

- "A la mujer, ni todo el dinero, ni todo el amor." / "To the woman, not all the money, nor all the love."
- "La mujer como la carabina, cargada y en la esquina." / "The woman should be like the carbine, loaded and in the corner."
- "La mujer es como el vino, engana al mas fino." / "The woman, like wine, fools the most fine."

The explicit and implicit messages about women are that they need to be controlled and "cornered." The same messages can also be found in specific songs sung when men are in pain about their loss of love, all further examples of oppresssion.

Mira como ando mujer por tu querer,
borracho y apasionado, no mas por tu amor,
Tu solo tu, eres causo de todo mi llanto
de mi desencanto y desesperacion.

Look how I am, woman,
Because of your love, drunk and impassioned
Only for your love,
You, only you
Have filled my life with sorrow
Opening a wound in my heart.

The songs, myths, stories, and poetry of colonial Latin America serve as a clear context for the learned behaviors of Hispanic Hacendados (plantation owners). The enslavement of the indigenous population is reflective in these proverbs and songs.

Cultural proverbs, songs, and the media, especially the telenovelas, or Spanish soap operas, contribute to the belief that men in Latino cultures are entitled to a double standard of living. It appears that the Mexican and American media are committed to the portrayal of Latino men as "sleazy." Antonio Banderas in *Desperado* and gangster films like *American Me* portray the image of a gang-banging, drug-dealing, violent-provoking predator.

The image of the Latino male as authoritarian, drunk, womanizing, and self-destructive has its psychological roots in Diaz-Guerrero et al.'s (1979), postulate that the Mexican male is a pelado, a raw individual behaving in an exaggerated superior, dominant manner.

"El hombre en la plaza y la mujer en la casa." / "While the man is in the plaza, the woman should be in her home."

These notions are explored in group process, when men in treatment describe those behaviors as reflective of "machismo." When the men are asked, what is a macho? they respond in the following manner: "El macho is violent, arrogant, savage, rebellious, stubborn, a womanizer, one who makes decisions on his own without consulting anyone." The Latino media are filled with images that in fact reinforce this blatant character of el macho. However, when the discussion is directed toward the learning of masculine behaviors in the native countries the men are from, el macho, in contrast, is portrayed in a completely different manner: "El macho is a man of his word, a responsible man, a provider, honest, respectful, admirable, humble, faithful, loyal to friends, family, and community, a man of integrity." Most men in treatment will agree that in the countries of origin, the previously described values are reflective of "macho" men.

In line with social learning and cognitive-behavioral principles, both behaviors and beliefs are presented to the men in treatment. They make their own decisions about where on the continuum, between the arrogant/violent "macho" and humble/noble "man/hombre," they are and where they want to be after treatment. The responsible man is reframed as the noble man or el hombre noble (Latino Men's Circle, 1992). The following empowerment intervention has been used in dealing with this issue.

Manuel and the other men in the group are asked the following question: "If your partner wants to go to work, do you let her, or does it not matter to you?"

Manuel responds, "I won't let her go to work." Other men reply, "I'll let her go to work." "I will give her permission to do so." The facilitator asks, "Who gave the right to determine her actions?" Where's the ownership title?" The facilitator reflects to the group that their responses are indicative of their oppressive attitude toward their partner and toward women in general. After all, states the facilitator, "Is it not the prerogative of the hacendado (plantation owner) to let his peons (slaves) work for him?" Manuel begins to contemplate this perspective. He begins to reflect on how in fact he had been treated as a child. His sisters were asked to "serve" him at mealtimes, and they or his mother made his bed. They greeted all of his friends as "special" family guests. Of course, he should feel entitled to exercise his superiority. He has expected this in all of his intimate relationships. Now, however, the perspective is being challenged by the group facilitator. Manuel realizes that he has in fact learned these behaviors and that he encourages his daughter to behave in the same way. Does that mean that she will marry someone who will treat her inequitably and/or violently? What does that mean for his identity, for his relationship with his partner, for his relationship with his children and the community at large?

The entire process requires a minimum of 16 weeks of psychoeducation that confronts patriarchal sexist ideology and teaches men safety, including timeout (el retiro) and responsible behaviors to arousal stimulation. In addition, a comparison of Western European patriarchial thinking and a Native American egalitarian worldview allows for a choice for the men in treatment. This prepares the clients for the third phase of treatment.

In view of this reality, the men are asked to prepare themselves to understand the spiritual dimension as it relates to balance, rhythm, and harmony (Latino Men's Circle, 1992). An ancient American indigenous ceremony is introduced at the juncture to help the men learn how to live in balance, rhythm, and harmony with "all of their relations" (Thin Elk, personal communication, February 12, 1992).

Manuel has now attended several group sessions. At the last session, he has been asked to reflect on what he would like to change in his life and/or solicit from the group process. He and the other group members are asked to bring a symbol of what they would like to leave behind or have more of. Manuel seriously ponders this and surprises the group with his "offering." He brings a wool glove filled with rocks. He states that this is symbolic of the violence he has perpetrated against his partner and wishes to stop. The group now is ready for the altar (el altar) ceremony.

THE ALTAR (EL ALTAR)

This ceremony is used extensively in the Americas to order one's life, to ask for balance, to live in rhythm and harmony with all of life's creation.

The concept of a higher power is introduced as it is known in the in-digenous worldview, the Creator. The prayer begins with an altar bear-ing the offerings from the group members and symbols for each of the four elements of life: fire, water, air, and earth. These elements are nec-essary for maintaining a balanced existence.

The men in the group stand in a circle and the prayer leader, the elder of the community, begins the prayer. The men face toward the east, the place of the Man, the Eagle, the place of illumination and clarity.

"Hacemos este ritual hoy para enfocarnos en el trabajo sagrado de parar nuestra violencia y para hacernos concientes de ganar entendimiento de porque somos violentos." ("Today we pray to focus our sacred labor to stop our violence and to become conscious of our understanding of why we are violent.")

"El Este es la direccion del Sol, del Aguila, y de el Hombre; le pedimos al poder superior, que nos de claridad para entender como vivir una vida sin violencia." ("The east is the direction of the Sun, the Eagle, and the Male Warrior. We ask the Creator to give us clarity to understand how we may live without violence.")

"El Oeste es la direccion del Oso, del Sueno, y de la Mujer. Le pedimos al ser superior que nos de valor para parar nuestra violencia y para hacernos consistes de como hemos lastimado a las personas con que hemos sido violentos. Tambien pedimos aprender como manjar nuestro coraje y dolor en una forma creativo para que no resulte en violencia." ("The West is the direction of the Bear, the Dream (Feeling Function), and the Woman. We ask the Creator for courage to stop our violence and to become more conscious of how we have hurt others with our vi-olence. We also ask to learn how to creatively direct our anger and pain without the use of violence.")

"El Sur es la direccion del Hogar de Los Ninos. Pedimos aprender a nu-trir a nuestro niño interno y ganar seguridad y confianza. Pedimos reco-brar nuestra expontaneidad natural y nuestra felicidad." ("The South is the home of the Children, of Trust, Innocence, and Creativity. We ask the Creator to teach us how to nurture our internal child with security and confidence. We ask to reclaim our natural spontaneity and happiness.")

"El Norte es la direccion de Los Ancianos y de experiencia. Pedimos en-contrar sabiduria para encontrar tranquilidad interna y establecer rela-ciones cooperativas con nuestras familiares y otras relaciones. Pedimos recobrar la relacion natural con nuestra voz intuitiva dentro de nosotros, para reponer una vida espiritual conciente." ("The North is the direction of the Elders, and Experience, Wisdom, and Understanding. We ask for tranquillity to reestablish cooperative relations with our family members and others. We ask to regain our intuition to respond to our spiritual consciousness.")

"El Centro es el punto convergente del cielo, el viento y la Madre Tierra, el lugar del movimiento y balance. Pedimos que nuestras vidas tengan balance para desarrollarnos como hombres Latinos." ("The Center is the direction of movement, balance, and harmony. It is the place where Mother Earth meets with the Wind and Father Sky. We ask to learn to live in rhythm, balance, and harmony.")*

Manuel shares that the prayer helps him order his world and gain control of his explosive behavior and obsessive thoughts, seek companionship with his group peers, and perform as a loving father. Although he is not religious, he appreciates the attention to the spiritual and recognizes that in his family background, there are shared beliefs about spirituality. There is an understanding that the spirit and the mind are related. The fact that Latino men are leading the prayer and the group process helps him accept these interventions.

PHASE 3: INTERNAL MOVEMENT OR PROCESS PSYCHOTHERAPY/INTEGRACION

Phase 3 reinforces the skills developed in the initial phases and incorporates the processing of the underlying clinical issues of dysfunctional behaviors. Concurrently, the relationship of the physiological, cognitive, and affective components of behavioral patterns are explored from a sociocultural and intergenerational perspective. The family constellation, familial patterns of loyalty, trust, and balance are explored in the current clinical environment (Boszormeny-Nagy & Krasner, 1986; Flores-Ortiz et al. 1994).

In addition, the effect of migration is explored, as well as the relationship between unresolved migratory experiences and the men's current psychological dysfunction (Cervantes, Synder & Padilla, 1989). Latino men have usually migrated to the United States for a variety of reasons: War-torn situations, unbearable poverty, unemployment, and natural catastrophes are just a few of the reasons given for moving to the United States The treatment protocol concentrates on a culture of support to allow the men an opportunity to express the psychological trauma experienced by them as a result of the mentioned clinical variables. Traumas requiring long-term exploration and healing include their own victimization from family violence, chaotic family backgrounds, a family history of alcoholism or chemical dependency, abrupt migration, post-traumatic stress

---

*Antonio Ramirez of Manalive recorded the prayer to fit the domestic violence group.

disorder (PTSD), real or imagined infidelities, and lost or absent fathers. However, this model does not support the traumatic experiences of the men as a justification for the violence.

The field of psychotherapy, especially the specialization of victimology, acknowledges the impact of trauma on the "spirit" of the client/victim (Madanes, 1990; Tello, 1992). Initial figures on offender's early victimization range from 60% to 90% (Sonkin, 1985; Walker, 1979). Our clinical experience confirms that at least 60% of the Latino men referred for treatment have been victims of maltreatment, and 20% are suffering from PTSD caused by traumatic migratory experiences or war-torn situations. These offenders are also "victims of trauma." Attention to their spirituality is essential to their healing and is an integrative aspect of their cultural heritage (Native American/Catholic/Christian/affiliation with Alcoholics Anonymous).

The emphasis of this phase is on the incorporation of prior learning in the previous phases of treatment. The men are asked to say how their family backgrounds have affected their current view of themselves, their partners, families, and work. Several issues also need to be addressed during this phase of the treatment protocol: the psychological impact of migration, the process of acculturation, the resolution of loss from family and friends, and their cultural environment.

Batterers have been described as suffering from social isolation (Caesar & Hamberger, 1989; Sonkin et al. 1985), immigrant batterers are more profoundly so (Carrillo & Marrujo, 1987). Therefore, group psychotherapy allows for the safe exploration of these suggested clinical variables.

> Manuel is asked to prepare his family tree for the group. In essence, the family tree is a family genogram of at least three generations. The group learns that he was raised in an alcoholic, extremely violent, chaotic family and that he migrated from Guatemala under political pressure of being killed. He returned home one day from the fields and found two male bodies dismembered at his doorstep; he thought they were his father and brother. His family asked him to leave immediately. If the facilitator had not asked him to present his family genogram, Manuel would not have informed the group of his close encounter with death. This explains the post-traumatic stress disorder symptoms he has demonstrated.

Post-traumatic stress disorder is present in many Latino therapy clients, especially those from Central America. One of the symptoms of PTSD is avoidance of the issues. It is imperative to explore to what extent the trauma is present if the client has migrated from a war-torn situation. Cognitive-behavioral techniques and reality-oriented matter-of-fact interventions have been found to be effective in dealing with this disorder in group process. New technology in the area of rapid eye movement desensitization appears to demonstrate promise (Shapiro, 1995).

Group psychotherapy requires a minimum of 6 months to deal with the above-mentioned clinical treatment variables. This is also a prerequisite in the family therapy phase, which requires both partners to assess the contingencies for dysfunctional as well as functional family behavioral patterns. A common example is the experience of an extramarital affair by the companera (partner). Men in therapy have tremendous difficulty in dealing with the confusion and pain that surround this event (Pittman, 1990). This is especially true for Latino domestic violence offenders. Batterers often use this as an excuse for the escalation of violence toward their partners.

> Manuel: "I can't get over how lousy I feel. I know I should just leave. Everyone is laughing at me, including my wife. I'd just like to leave and return to Guatemala, but I know I can't. I just can't take her making me a buey (cuckold). She's making it with my brother."

> Jose: "I remember when that happened to me. In Nicaragua, my wife had an affair. I just could not believe it. I was an excellent provider; she had everything she needed, the children were taken care of, but after analyzing the situation, I found that I was responsible for her affair. I was never at home. I was drinking, womanizing, and doing whatever I wanted to do. She needed the comfort and warmth of a companion who understood her. I wasn't providing that."

Clinical experience and empirical research demonstrate that batterers are extremely insecure and psychologically fragile (Carrillo, 1985). In cases of lethality, where one spouse has murdered another or the frequency and severity of the violence has escalated to dangerous levels, the real or imagined loss of the relationship is perceived as life threatening to the batterer. "I can't live without her," many have stated. This is a period of high risk, and extreme caution on the part of the clinician is urged. Therefore, the loss of the relationship needs to be broached with this point in mind. Not all Latino families reconcile during treatment, nor should all do so if the threat of violence continues.

> The group focuses on the reason why women may need to leave a relationship. The men are confronted by the way dysfunctional behaviors affect their partners and are shown how the "dance" of the relationship is an act of balance. Dysfunctional interactions among marital partners is common in domestic violence situations (Neidig & Friedman, 1984). Power, hurt, pain, helplessness, and hopelessness are common therapeutic issues. The men learn to accept that the reparation of the spiritual

violence requires their listening to the pain experienced by the partner at their own hands. They learn to hear the deep wounds relayed by their children as they watched their father beat their mother. In the group psychotherapy process, the men begin their preparation for the "men's work" of hearing out their families' psychological trauma resulting from the violence at their own hands.

Manuel appears to be ready for family therapy. However, before leaving the group, a final ceremony is introduced for the termination of the group experience. Manuel is asked to prepare a dish for the group. He brings pepian, a traditional dish from his country. The group is prepared for the final session that Manuel will attend. We call this ceremony La Dispedida/Saying Goodbye with Dignity. The men in the group share one real experience for which they are grateful to Manuel. He in turn shares what he has learned from each and every group member. Manuel is now an elder of the community. He gives a final consejo, vignette of wisdom, some sage advice to the new group members about participating in the group process. He then feeds the group and makes the first family therapy appointment, after consulting with his partner. He is invited to return as a volunteer/elder/advocate for the newcomers to the group.

PHASE 4: INTEGRATED MOVEMENT OR COMPLETION OF THE HEALING CIRCLE/MOVIMIENTO

Phase 4 embraces the entire family to provide the support to heal from the multiple traumas experienced by men's violence. The model for family therapy is Contextual/Strategic Family Therapy (Flores-Ortiz et al. 1994; Madanes, 1990), which has proven to be effective with Latinos suffering from some of these dysfunctional intergenerational behavioral patterns (Bernal et al. 1986). The treatment emphasis is the reestablishment of trust, repentance, and reparation for the spiritual, physical, and psychological damage accrued by the other family members. Safety to victim(s) continues to be primary in this treatment protocol. The heart of this phase is the reestablishment of balance. A variety of ceremonies The Altar/El Altar, Family Tree/Arbol (the family genogram); The Movie/La Novela (Aguilar, 1972; Sinclair, 1990), and The Farewell with Dignity/La Despedida, have all been utilized and hopefully incorporated into the clients' behavioral repertoire for recovery.

The use of ceremony, spirituality, symbols, and metaphor is well documented in the literature (Aguilar, 1972; Alcoholics Anonymous, 1921;

Jung, 1964; Madanes, 1990). The symbols, language, stories, myths, music, poetry, and ceremonies used in this treatment protocol are indigenous to precolumbian, Native American, Latino, Hispanic, and Chicano peoples. This allows for unfreezing/descongelamiento of dysfunctional thoughts and behaviors that contribute to the violent behavior of the offender.

Madanes (1990) noted that "all problems brought to therapy can be said to stem from the dilemma between love and violence. This dilemma appears in different dimensions: the fear of a struggle for power, as the desire to be loved, as the despair of not being able to love and protect, and as the shame of not repenting and not loving compassionately. . . . When love has deteriorated into violence," the therapist encourages the violent family member to accept blame and to repent (p. 50). The entire treatment process has prepared the men to handle the painful recollections of their family members. They are expected to repent for the physical, psychological, sexual, and spiritual violence that they have caused their family. They also are challenged to continuously work in preventing relapse. The family, in turn, is directed to develop strategies to prevent further violence and to ensure the protection of its members (Madanes, 1990).

Flores-Ortiz et al. (1995) defined the treatment protocol for Latino families involved in the pain of family violence, sexual abuse, and chemical dependency. The theoretical perspective takes into account four different dimensions: facts, individual psychology (thoughts, feelings, motivations; for immigrants, migration experiences), interactional processes, and what Boszormeny-Nagy & Spark (1974) define as "relational justice."

The first dimension covers the facts: physical characteristics, age, ethnicity, income level, religious practices, country of origin, education, and for the families in the clinical case examples; the intergenerational history of abuse (physical, sexual, psychological) and chemical dependency.

The second dimension, individual psychology, attends to the contribution of individual family members to the system. It covers personality characteristics, the expression of emotionality, and conflict resolution. This model requires the careful assessment of depression, the potential for suicide/homicide, as well as the spiritual capacity for pain resolution.

The third dimension, interactional processes, is concerned with the structure of the family, intergenerational patterns, boundaries, roles, and hierarchy. Families with domestic violence have developed rigid patterns of behavior based on modeling, traditional sex role expectations, and acceptance of violence as a form of conflict resolution. Dysfunctional (pain-filled) patterns exist in these families that are evident in the chronic repetition of the use of chemicals, abuse, and poverty. Frozen patterns/conjelados that may have resulted in the migratory process also need to be considered.

The final dimension of analysis, of "relational justice," is concerned with the ethical relations of family members resulting from merits and rights on the one hand, and debts and obligations on the other. Balance is a key concept here. Balanced relations are considered ethical and just in this model. It becomes apparent with violent chemical-dependent families that relations are chronically and painfully imbalanced. Therapy and a major change in behavior can assist with the rebalancing of the family "ledger." Part of the therapeutic task in assisting the rebalancing of the family ledger is to direct the reparation and rebuilding of the family circle. (Tello, 1992).

The task of the therapy is to re-root the family in their destiny/destino, which is what having a good cara/face is about in precolumbian cultures. Family roles must be re-established that are not rigid or frozen. Despite the fact that these families must have firm boundaries and expectations/ reglas firmes, the therapist must be careful not to reproduce the rigid patterns of imbalance that exist in these families.

New traditions and ceremonies must be developed with the family that allow for a celebration of a new existence with and among the family members. Previously violent men need a support group of men who are not afraid to reject violence in their communities. Compadres con Palabra (National Compadres Network, 1995) is an example of men who are committed to the reparation of violence in their communities and who are willing to mentor young men as bridge builders in the rites of passage for noblement/"hombres nobles."

In summary, the treatment of the Latino offender, as with all batterers, requires thorough diagnostics, tailored treatment plans, and needs assessments to include the batterer's family. An emphasis on the values of respect, dignity, trust, and love articulated in their own language and cultural milieu can contribute to successful rapport building. It is imperative that the effects of colonialization, racism, discrimination, and migration also be addressed in treatment. Our preference is that the treatment focus be systemic and intergenerational, including as much of the family as possible, whenever it is safe to do so.

In order to perform works of healing, one must respect the clients' worldview. This particular treatment model is a small contribution to the field of the cessation of family violence. It is the strength of the family that has survived several periods of colonialization for Latinos on this continent. In the spirit of resistance to the colonialization of Hispanic cultures, it is our contention that, although family violence is internalized oppression is expressed toward its members. It is the family circle that can help heal the community and contribute to the healing of the greater disordered society from its many wounds of oppression.

REFERENCES AND BIBLIOGRAPHY

Arrom, S. M. (1978). *Women! The family in Mexico City, 1800–1867*. Doctoral dissertation. Stanford University.

Baca-Zinn, M. (1979). Chicano men and masculinity. *Journal of Ethnic Studies, 10*, 2.

Bandura, A. (1973). *Aggression: A social learning analysis*. Englewood Cliffs, NJ: Prentice-Hall.

Baron, L., & Strauss, M. (1988). Cultural and economic sources of homicide in the United States. *The Sociological Quarterly, 29*, 371–390.

Beck, A. T. (1976). *Cognitive therapy and the emotional disorders*. New York: International Universities Press.

Bernal, G., Flores-Ortiz, Y., & Rodriguez-Draguin, C. (1986). Terapia familiar intergeneracional con Chicanos y familias Mejicanas inmigrantes a Los Estados Unidos. *Cuadernos de Sicologia, 8*, 81–99.

Boszormeny-Nagy, I., & Krasner, B. R. (1986).

Boszormeny-Nagy, I., & Krasner, B. R. (1979). Trust based therapy: A contextual approach. *American Journal of Psychiatry, 137*, 767–775.

Boszormeny-Nagy, I. & Spark, G. M. (1974). *Invisible loyalties*. New York: Harper & Row.

Brice-Baker , J. R. (1994). Domestic violence in African American and African Carribean families. *Journal of Social Distress and the Homeless, 3*(1), 23–38.

Browne, A. (1986). When battered women kill. New York: The Free Press.

Bureau of the Census. Persons of Spanish origin in the United States (Current Population Reports, Series P-29).

Butterfield, F. (1995). All God's children: The basket family and the American tradition of violence. New York: Alfred Knopf.

Caesar, P. L., & Hamberger, K. L. (Eds.). (1989). Treating men who batter: Theory, practice, and programs. New York: Springer.

Caetano, R. (1983). Drinking patterns and alcohol problems among Hispanics in the U.S.: A review. *Drug and Alcohol Dependence, 12*(1), 37–59.

Carrillo, R. A. (1985). The male batterer: A social learning and multivariate analysis. In E. Nebelkoff & A. Alcompora (Eds.), *Proceedings of the World Congress of Therapeutic Communities.*
Bridging services: Drug abuse, human services and the therapeutic community. San Francisco: Walden House.

Carrillo, R. A., & Marrujo, B. (1987). *Acculturation and domestic violence in the Hispanic community*. Paper presented at the Second National Conference on Family Violence, University of New Hampshire.

Cervantes, N. N., & Cervantes, J. M. (1993). A multi-cultural perspective in the treatment of domestic violence. In M. Hansen & M. Harway (Eds.), *Battering and family therapy: A feminist perspective* (pp 156–174). Newbury Park, CA: Sage Publications.

Cervantes, R. C., Algado de Snyner, V. N., & Padilla, A. M. (1989). Post-traumatic stress symptoms among immigrants from Central America and Mexico. *Journal of Hospital and Community Psychiatry.*

Coleman, D. H., & Straus, M. A. (1987). Marital power, conflict, and violence in a nationally representative sample of American couples. *Violence and Victims, 1*, 141–157.

Crillio, S., & DiBlasio (1992). *Families that abuse: Diagnosis and therapy*. New York: Norton.

Diaz-Guerrero, R., Lichtszajn, J. L., & Reyes, L. I. (1979). Alienacion de la madre, psicopatologia y la practica clinica en Mexico. *Hispanic Journal of Behavioral Sciences, 1*, 117–133.

Dutton, D. G. (1988). *The domestic assault of women: Psychological and criminal justice perspectives.* Boston: Allyn Bacon.

Figley, C. (1978). *Stress disorders among Vietnam veterans.* New York: Brunner/Mazel.

Flores-Ortiz, Y., & Carrillo, R. A. (1989). *La violencia en la familia: Un modelo contextual de terapia intergeneracional.* Paper presented at the Congresso Interamericana de Sicologia, Buenos Aires.

Flores-Ortiz, Y., Esteban, M., & Carrillo, R. A. (1994). La violencia en la familia: Un modelo contextual de terapia intergeneracional. *Revista InterAmericana de Psicologia/Interamerican Journal of Psychology, 28*(2), 235–250.

Freire, P. (1972). *Pedagogy of the oppressed.* New York: Herder & Herder.

Gelles, R., & Straus, M. (1988). The cost of family violence: Preliminary results from a national survey.

Goldner, V., Walter, G., Penn, P., & Wienberg, M. (1992). Love and violence: Gender paradoxes in volatile attachments. Miami: AAMFT Conference.

Gondolf, E. (1985). Men who batter: An integrated approach for stopping wife abuse. Holmes Beach, FL: Learning Publications.

Gondolf, E. (1988). How some men stop their abuse: An exploratory program evaluation. In G. T. Hotaling, D. Finkelhor, J. T. Kirkpatrick, & M. A. Strauss. (Eds.), Coping with family violence. Newbury Park, CA: Sage.

Gondolf, E. (1990). *Psychiatric response to family violence: Identifying and confronting neglected danger.* Lexington Books.

Griswold-Del Castillo, R. (1984). La familia: Chicano families in the urban southwest, 1848 to the present. Notre Dame, IN: University of Notre Dame Press.

Hampton, R. L. (1987). *Violence in the Black family: Correlates and consequences.* Lexington Books.

Laslett, B. (1975). Household structure on an American frontier: Los Angeles, California, in 1850. *American Journal of Sociology, 81*(1), 109–128.

Laslett, Barbara (1977). Social change and the family: Los Angeles, California, 1850–1870. *American Sociological Review, 42*(2), 269–290.

Latino Men's Circle. (1992). *Reflections of the Latino male.* Los Angeles

Levinson, D. (1989). Family violence in crosscultural perspective. Newbury Park, CA: Sage Publications.

Loftin, C., & Hill, R. H. (1974). Regional subculture and homicide: An examination of the Gastil-Hackney thesis. *American Sociological Review, 39*, 714–724.

Madanes, (1990). Sex, love and violence. New York: Gardner Press.

Martin, D. (1981). Battered wives. San Francisco: Volcano Press.

Marin, G., Sabogal, F., Marin, B. V., Otero-Sabogal, R. & Perez-Stable, E. J. (1986). Cultural values and acculturation among Hispanics (Technical Report No. 3, Hispanic Smoking Cessation Research Project).

Marin, G., Sabogal, F., Marin, B. V., Otero-Sabogal, R. & Perez-Stable, E. J. (1987). Development of a short acculturation scale for Hispanics. *Hispanic Journal of Behavioral Sciences, 9*(2), 183–205.

Margolin, G. (1987). The multiple forms of aggressiveness between marital partners: How do we identify them? A longitudinal investigation. *Journal of Family Violence, 3*, 73–87.

Meichenbaum, D. (1977). *Cognitive behavior therapy.* New York: Plenum.

Minuchin, S., & Elizue V. (1990). *Institutionalization madness*. New York: Bosie Books.

Mirandé, A., & Enriquez, E. (1979). *La Chicana: The Mexican-American woman*. Chicago and London: University of Chicago Press.

Neff, J. A., Holamon, B., & Schluter, T. D. (1995). Spousal violence among Anglos, Blacks and Mexican Americans: The role of demographic variables, psychosocial predictions, and alcohol consumption. *Journal of Family Violence, 10*(1), 1–21.

Neidieg, P. T. & Friedman, D. (1984). *Spousal abuse: A treatment program for couples*. Champagne, IL: Research Press.

O'Leary, D., & Curley, A. D. (1986). Assertion and family violence: Correlates of spouse abuse. *Journal of Marital and Family Therapy, 3*, 281–289.

Padilla, A. (Ed). (1980). *Acculturation: Theory, models and some new findings*. Boulder, CO: Westview Press.

Pagelow, M. D. (1981). *Women battering: Victims and their experience*. Beverly Hills, CA: Sage.

Penalosa, R. (1986). *Central Americans in Los Angeles*. Los Angeles: UCLA, Spanish Speaking Mental Health Research Center.

Pence, E., & Paymar, M. (1993). *Education groups for men who batter: The Duluth model*. New York: Springer.

Pizzey, E. (1974). *Scream quietly or the neighbors will hear you*. London: Penguin.

Rosenbaum, A., & O'Leary, D. K. (1981). Marital violence: Characteristics of abusive couples. *Journal of Consulting and Clinical Psychology, 49*, 63–71.

Saunders, D. G. & Parker, J. C. (1989). Legal sanctions and treatment follow through among men who batter: A multivariant analysis. *Social Work Research and Abstracts, 25*(3), 21–29.

Sinclair, H.(1990). *An accountable/advocacy batterer intervention program*. San Rafael, CA: Manalive.

Sluzky, C., & Ranson, D. (Eds.). (1976). *Double bind: The foundation of communicational approach to the family*. New York: Grune & Stratton; London: Academic Press.

Sonkin, D. J., & Durphy, M. (1989). *Learning to live without violence: A handbook for men*. San Francisco: Volcano Press.

Sonkin, D. J., Martin, D., & Walker, L. E. A. (1985). *The male batterer: A treatment approach*. New York: Springer.

Sorenson, S. B., & Telles, C. A. (1987, September). *Family violence in immigrant and non-immigrant Hispanics in Los Angeles*. Paper presented at the Research Conference on Violence and Homicide in Hispanic Communities. UCLA, Los Angeles.

Straus, M., Gelles, R., & Stienmetz, S. (1980). *Behind closed doors: Violence in the American family*. New York: Doubleday / Anchor.

Strauss M. A., & Smith, C. (1989). Violence in Hispanic families in the United States: Incidence rates and structural interpretations. In M. A. Strauss & R. J. Gelles. (Ed.), Physical violence in American families: Risk factors and adaptations to violence in 8,145 families. New Brunswick, NJ: Transaction Press.

Szapocznik, J., Scopetta, M. A., Kurtines, W., & de Los Angeles, Arnalde, M. (1984). Theory and measurement of acculturation. *Interamerican Journal of Psychology*.

Szapocznik, J. Santisteban, D., Kurtines, W., Perez-Vidal, A., & Hervis, O. (1983, November). *Bicultural effectiveness training: A treatment intervention for enhancing intercultural adjustment in Cuban American families*. Paper presented at Ethnicity, Acculturation and Mental Health among Hispanics Conference. Albuquerque, NM.

Tello, J. (1992). *Cara y corazon*. Los Angeles: Suenos Publications.

Vega, W. A., & Miranda, M. R. (1985). Hispanic mental health: Relating research to service. Rockville, MD.

Walker, L. (1979). The battered woman. New York: Harper & Row.

Walker, L. (1989). Terrifying love: Why battered women kill and how society responds. Grand Rapids, MI: Harper & Row.

Walker, L. E. (1984). The battered woman syndrome. New York: Springer.

Williams, O. J. (1994). Group work with African American men who batter: Toward more ethnically sensitive practice. *Journal of Comparative Family Studies, 25*, 91–103.

Ybarra, L. (1977). *Conjugal role relationships in the Chicano family*. Unpublished doctoral dissertation University of California, Berkeley.

4

Healing and Confronting the African American Male Who Batters

Oliver J. Williams

FISH IN A BARREL

Once there was a scientist who studied the health and behavior of fish. To track the health status of the fish on a consistent basis, the scientist went to the ocean, caught 12 fish, and put them in a barrel. Over time he noticed that one of the fish developed a spot on its back fin. He recorded its occurrences and noted this was unusual for this type of fish. A few days passed, and more fish developed spots and became ill. Eventually, all but one fish developed a spot in the same location and got sick. After numerous efforts to treat the fish, the illness would not go away. The scientist concluded that the fish without symptoms was immune to the disease; the other fish were unhealthy and the disease emanated from them. Because few scientists studied this type of fish, he considered himself to be an expert, and deemed the illness-free fish as the standard for fish of its kind. All descriptions defining the normal state of being for this type of fish were modeled from the scientist's report.

The "normal" fish was eventually set aside in its own container. To cross-check his results, the scientist returned to the ocean, caught 12 more fish, and put them in a barrel; the same thing happened. This time, two fish were without symptoms. The scientist concluded that these fish had become contaminated and issued a report to the public that "until further notice, these fish are unsafe." The cause of the illness and the key to immunity were unknown.

Another scientist, concerned with the health of the fish, sought to determine the reason for the illness. He posited that the community of fish and natural environments may have been protective factors. Fish tend to

74

flourish in environments that match their natural capacities. The barrel represented a change that the fish could not negotiate. One potential healing approach was to return the fish to their natural environment, but this could result in more contaminated fish. A second approach was to create another healthy environment and community of fish that simulated the ocean conditions. The second option was selected, and the fish were restored to health.

INTRODUCTION

Violence in intimate partner relationships is a crime that results in the injury or death of thousands of women each year. Although pro-arrest policies, jail time and group treatment have emerged as approaches to confront men who batter, strategies must be developed to encourage more of these men to take responsibility for their destructive behavior.

It is incumbent for those who work in this field to expand the way in which they view the causes and solutions to partner abuse. Current interventions in partner abuse treatment are often defined by theories of violence arising out of a singular point of view. These theories tend to promote a one-size-fits-all perspective and do not account for all of the important intersection of race, culture and violence (Williams and Becker, 1995). This is especially true regarding African American men who batter. Men of color, as a group, drop out of treatment sooner and complete treatment at lower rates than their white counterparts (Saunders & Parker, 1989; Tolman & Bennett, 1990). The present theories that explain male violence in partner relationships ignore key explanations for maladaptive behavior among African American men. Yet both conventional partner abuse and culturally-focused perspectives provide important information about abusive behavior in intimate partner relationships involving African American men. This chapter will examine the theories that explain violence in the field of partner abuse and those that address maladaptive behavior among African American men. From these suppositions, this chapter will highlight a theoretical framework for designing appropriate and culturally-congruent treatment interventions for African American men who batter.

EXPLANATION FOR VIOLENCE IN THE PARTNER ABUSE LITERATURE

The battered women's movement has helped scholars, researchers and practitioners understand that theory and practice must be modeled around the lives of those who are most affected by violence: battered women. This grass-roots movement has raised our society's consciousness to the problem of domestic violence on many levels. It has produced battered women's shelters, informed society about the impact of family violence on children, and was instrumental in the creation of treatment for men who batter (Westra & Martin, 1981; Edleson & Eisikovits, 1996; Pele, 1996).

The battered women's movement and a feminist critique of theories of violence have shaped the explanations for male battering behavior (NRC, 1996) as well. Two theories seem to stand out from this literature: structural theory as it relates to sexism, and the theory of learned behavior. From a feminist perspective of structural theory, violence toward women is explained in terms of gender in equality (Yllo, 1988). It has been viewed as a symptom of another problem, sexism, which is the devaluation and subordination of women by men (Rothenberg, 1988). Historically, sexism has been embodied in laws and cultural norms, which have given men license to be abusive toward women physically, emotionally, economically and legally (Oppenlandar, 1981). In a review of mainstream history concerning partner abuse, laws have typically been a hindrance to women's capacity to address this problem; and they implicitly and explicitly support male violence. Until recently, there have been few sanctions for partner abuse. Violence is a choice men who batter make because the benefit is control; the results are immediate; and the legal consequences, historically, have been minimal. Ellen Pence (1989) explains how men use power and control in intimate relationships. She has influenced many in the field of domestic violence through her explanation of violence toward women. Gondolf (1985) also supports that a shared characteristic among men who batter is their need to control their female partner. Although some researchers suggest that violence for certain men also can be influenced by physical illness or personality disorders, most in the field acknowledge that the abuse of women is perpetrated by men who appear, in other ways as typical of men in society (Sonkin, Martin, and Walker, 1985; Saunders, 1992; Gondolf, 1988; Holtzworth-Munroe and Stuart, 1994; Roy, 1982). From this perspective, abuse is not considered merely a random act but a behavior focused specifically on a female partner. Currently, the protection of women and development of laws that will hold men who batter accountable for their abusive behavior have been major objectives of the battered women's movement.

According to the theory of learned behavior, violence is taught in relationships among members of a subgroup or community. When a person witnesses violence in a community or subgroup setting, they may imitate the behavior in anger considering it a normal strategy to employ in conflict situations. Once the behavior is learned, it is passed on from generation to generation (Bandura, Ross, and Ross, 1963; Berkowitz, 1983; Rich and

Stone, 1996; Rosenberg and Mercy, 1991; and Hammond and Yung, 1993). In the field of domestic violence, scholars specifically describe what behaviors men have learned and how their abusive behavior is directed toward women (Straus, 1978; Gelles, 1979; Martin, 1976; Flynn, 1977; Steinmetz, 1980). Violence is considered a male prerogative (Straus, 1980; Williams, 1989). Male socialization tends to make men, as a group, more accepting of violence (David and Brannon, 1976; Cicone and Ruble, 1978). Much of the research suggests that partner abuse is learned within the family of origin. In many cases, young boys who observe their mother being abused by an adult male role model are at higher risk to abuse their female partners as adults (Lewis et al., 1979). In batterers' treatment groups, some of the themes of treatment include the following: developing male alternatives to violence, increasing perpetrators' awareness of their need to control and reducing their sexist attitudes and behavior. One clear message from the field is that men who batter must be accountable for their behavior. Another is that men who behave poorly toward their partner are at higher risk for abusing or alienating others, e.g. children, other family members, neighbors, and colleagues. Often group treatment encourages personal awareness, responsibility and accountability. Although this perspective is important and, in my opinion, must be a primary focus of treatment, scholars and practitioners must integrate such explanations with other realities including social context and cultural experiences.

AFRICAN AMERICAN MALE PERSPECTIVES ON MALADAPTIVE BEHAVIOR

The intersections of race, social status and violence creates a set of issues that has typically not been discussed in the literature on domestic violence (Williams, 1994). Few theories are specific regarding partner abuse among African American men. In fact, scholars who explore theories of African American men and maladaptive behaviors select this group due to their high rates of suicide, homicide and acquaintance violence rather than their involvement with partner violence.

Among the explanations for maladaptive behaviors in African American men, two theories stand out: structural theory and interactional theory. In these theories, scholars explore the experiences of young African American men either in racist and oppressive or violent social environments. They report that an oppressive social environment encourages violence (Blake and Darling, 1994; Hammond and Yung, 1993; Hawkins, 1987; Lemelle, 1995; Oliver, 1994; Rich and Stone, 1996; Roberts, 1994; Taylor-Gibbs, 1988; Williams and Griffin, 1991; and Wilson, 1992).

Many African American men are uniquely affected by violent social environments. Homicide is the leading cause of death among African American men ages 15 to 34; they also have high rates of acquaintance violence and suicide. African Americans are more at risk for physical harm by other African Americans than by Whites, and vice versa (Blake and Darling, 1994; Hammond and Yung, 1993; Hawkins, 1987; Rich and Stone, 1996; Roberts, 1994). Trey Ellis, in a work entitled, "What Does it Feel Like to be a Problem?" comments on the plight of African American men in society. In order to intervene with these men he makes the following observation:

> Ironically, African American men have more right than anyone else to run and hide when other black men head our way on the sidewalk. Yet, we don't (most of us anyway), because we bother to separate the few bad from the legion of good. . . . I'm not making excuses for the black criminal—I despise him for poisoning and shooting more of my people than the cowardly Klan ever did. But we need to understand him as a human being if we're ever going to save him, or at least, save his younger brother or his son (Ellis, 1995).

Writers who are concerned about maladaptive behaviors in African American men attempt to discern the social realities and antecedents that produce this behavior among these men without excusing their negative behavior. There is a convergence of opinions among many scholars that African American men are not the sole cause of their destructive behaviors. In fact, many scholars imply that to understand African American male deviance, it is imperative to understand white societal oppression. An oppressive structural social context creates hostile living environments that produce a range of maladaptive reactions among some African American men. The violence that results is predictable. Staples (1982) and Taylor-Gibbs (1988) note that violence toward women may be one maladaptive behavior that results, although most of the writers in this area chronicle other forms of interpersonal violence and problem behaviors.

STRUCTURAL THEORY AND AFRICAN AMERICAN'S MALADAPTIVE RESPONSES

Staples (1982) and Wilson (1992) suggest that before one can truly understand violence perpetrated by African American males, there must be a critique of the African American man's experience in the United States. Violence in the lives of African Americans is allowed and even promoted because historically their lives have been devalued in American society (Hawkins, 1987). It is, therefore, imperative to recognize the types of societal violence he experiences to understand the violence some African

American men perpetrate (Wilson, 1992). Violence and oppression unleashed on African Americans every day goes unnamed (Gary, 1995; Lemelle, 1994; Staples, 1982; Taylor-Gibbs, 1988; Wilson, 1992). Wilson (1992) observes the following:

> The physical and psychological violence of White America against Black America which began with Afrikan slavery in America has continued to this moment in a myriad of forms: wage slavery and peonage; economic discrimination and warfare; political-economic disenfranchisement; Jim Crowism; general White hostility and Klan terrorism; lynching; injustice and "legal lynching," the raping of Black women and the killing of Black men by whites which have gone unredressed by the justice system; the near-condoning and virtual approval of Black-on-Black violence, differential arrest, criminal indictments and incarceration . . . segregation; job, business, professional and labor discrimination; negative stereotyping and character assassination; housing discrimination; police brutality; addictive drug importation; poor and inadequate education; inadequate and often absent health care; inadequate family support, etc. (p. 7)

Lemelle (1995) states that the study of African American male deviant behavior highlights the individual's relationship to production. He argues that the study of "Black male deviance" should focus on the organization of labor under capitalism. This requires an examination of U.S. social and cultural history viewed from the perspective of class struggle. A societal structure built on a dominator/subordinate model seeks to maintain the status quo where African Americans are the subordinate group and part of the underclass. In this context, the values of the dominator are to be internalized and reinforced, while the values of the subordinates are devalued and rejected (Lemelle, 1995; Roberts, 1994). African Americans become frustrated attempting to follow all the rules while still facing the barriers of discrimination (Chestang, 1993).

Oppressive experiences faced by African Americans occur within a sustaining environment. In sustaining environments, African Americans earn a living, are educated, obtain goods and services and are involved in other activities that support their capacity to exist in society. They also must endure institutional racism and other forms of oppression in such environments. In contrast, a nurturing environment could be counted on to assist most African Americans in negotiating societal oppression, discrimination and racism, in all its forms (Chestang, 1976 and Norton, 1978). This nurturing environment consists of African American families, media, neighborhoods, churches and community. During the 1970s, the African American community could rely on the presence of a nurturing environment. Since that time, the level of violence has increased significantly.

Today many of the social supports that had constituted the nurturing environment have eroded (Taylor-Gibb, 1988). Many mobile African Americans (working class, middle class and educated) left the former segregated neighborhoods and moved to integrated environments. This created a greater gap in economic diversity, advocacy programs, role models, social supports, social networks, community leadership and a greater gap between middle class and poor African Americans. The results created increasingly stressful community and living environments, with fewer supports and resources for those who were left behind. Furthermore, these environments were at increased risk for poverty, stress, frustration, crime and violence.

It should also be noted, however, that the gap in social support could be experienced by those who left, as well as those who were left behind. Although more mobile African Americans had greater financial resources, they were not necessarily connected to enriched family or community support, and advocacy. All African American males experience social oppression regardless of social status, but low-income men may feel it more intensely (Gary, 1995). Any African American male who is not connected to a healthy nurturing support system is at risk for displaying maladaptive responses.

AFRICAN AMERICAN MEN
AND INTERACTIONAL THEORY

One consequence of an oppressive societal context is stressful and violent community environments that foster violent interactions among men. Nicholson (1996) and McCall (1994) describe their experiences in violent African American community environments and explain that violence was a behavioral imperative among their peers. They further explain that to move away from violence was a personal struggle and evolution to self awareness. Rich & Stone (1996) describe the meaning of "being a sucker" for young African American male victims and perpetrators of violence. They interviewed African American men in hospital emergency rooms who were victims of violence. Respondents reported that either an unwillingness to use violence or the perception of "weakness" and vulnerability could result in more danger and increase the potential for abuse, more so than the actual use of violence. Oliver (1994) describes the tough-guy personality that develops from exposure to a violent environmental context. Violence may ensue based on one's perceptions of others, within this context. Such perceptions can be triggered by verbal and nonverbal interactions with others. What is important to recognize is that most people in that environment are operating on the same set of cognitive and behavioral imperatives. Violence for some is viewed as a rule for living and/or survival. The attributions for violence are then generalized to other contexts, such as family or intimate relationships (Williams, 1994). Violent behavior, therefore, may result from either a reaction to oppression or through learned behavior from a hostile and violent community environment. Williams and Griffin, (1991) suggest that the violence that results can be directed at the self, at intimate relationships or at the community (see Figure 4.1).

BLENDING CONVENTIONAL WISDOM WITH AN AFRICAN AMERICAN MALE PERSPECTIVE

Separately, theories concerning partner abuse or maladaptive behaviors and African American males offer only partial explanations concerning the behavior of African American men who batter. Regarding domestic violence, sexism, male socialization and social learning are the underlying conditions for violence; controlling and abusive behavior are the results. Legal accountability is used to sanction and control maladaptive behaviors. Group treatment is a method used to reform and educate men who batter. Societal and internalized oppression and a violent social learning environment can produce a range of maladaptive behaviors in African American men. These maladaptive behaviors can include problems such as crime, substance abuse, and violence. Several writers in this field suggest that such behaviors require holistic treatment. Instead of focusing on isolated behavior change with individual behavior problems, more could be accomplished through healing and teaching African American men to live a balanced life within a community of self and others (Akabar, 1989; Blake and Darling, 1994). Men who are emotionally out of balance tend to substitute one maladaptive behavior for another (Blake and Darling, 1994). Other researchers recommend that attention to the African American males' social realities is imperative. Violent African American men must develop skills to negotiate racist and violent oppressive situations and environments in adaptive ways (Williams, in press). Nicholson (1994) and McCall (1996) describe a time in which they did not see violence as a choice but eventually learned that there were alternatives to violence. Taylor-Gibbs (1988) and Wilson (1992) recommend sanctions for the negative behavior, but they also suggest providing resource and development information for men who live in highly stressed urban communities. Treatment approaches with violent African American men must make the link between the oppression they experience and the oppression they perpetuate because violence toward women may be a result of displaced anger from their social

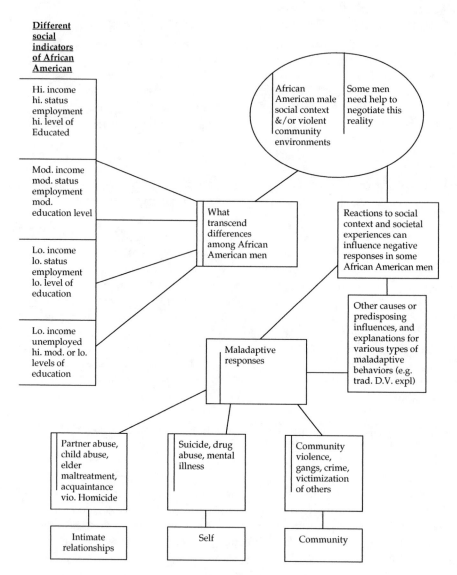

FIGURE 4.1   Effects of oppression on African American men.

context (Williams, 1993; Wilson, 1992). Taken together, the two theoretical perspectives provide greater insight on multiple levels in understanding and responding to men who batter. A broader, integrated perspective on violence encourages the development of more effective treatment intervention. Presently, there is no language to discuss the blending of these perspectives. Those who write about domestic violence usually do not refer to the work of scholars of African American maladaptive behaviors, and vice verse. In order to effectively confront male battering in this population, practitioners and researchers must become familiar with the literature of both fields. Models of practice with African American men who batter must emerge from these combined theories (refer to Figure 4.2).

WHAT SHOULD A BLENDED PERSPECTIVE EMPHASIZE?

Because there is not a common reality between the two fields of violence, it is truly a challenge to address the question of what a blended perspective should emphasize. The question itself sparks a debate because the perspectives on what is most important differs so drastically based on the perception of needs. Clearly the safety of women is paramount. Those who work with female victims of domestic violence understand all too well the nature and behavior of men who batter. They also demand that the destruction done to women every day must be addressed. To listen to women's stories

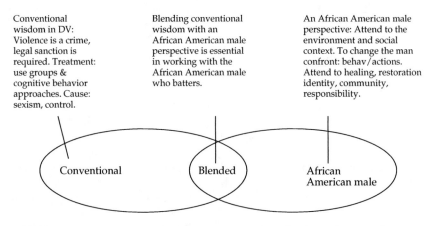

FIGURE 4.2 Demonstrating how conventional methods must be blended with an African American male perspective.

about their abuse and humiliation and the realities of their experiences helps one recognize that sanctions and accountability are essential to stop maladaptive behaviors from continuing and to send a message that such behavior is not allowed. In contrast, those who work with African American men see boys and men either hurt or dying at the hands of other men. They also see the destruction and the breeding ground for anger and hostility. They, too, ask the question of primary interest in partner abuse: How do you stop people from re-abusing, and how do you prevent men from ever starting violent and abusive behavior? Although sanctions and jail time is one response, it cannot be the only response. Sanctions must be a consequence of maladaptive behaviors. However, a theme among scholars who write about violence among African American men refer to a type of healing that is essential in order for change to occur. But the notion of sanctions plus healing appear to be unlikely partners. The debate over punishment versus rehabilitation in criminal justice is a similar conflict. Given the nature of the problem, helpers must find a way to make it work. The realities of battered women and African American men are important. For change to occur, it is imperative that we don't get caught in a zero-sum perspective. The debate must center on a framework of inclusion. The message that must be sent to African American men, as well as all men who batter, that destructive behavior is not acceptable and changing such behaviors is desirable.

A common philosophy must emerge between scholars and practitioners in the partner abuse field and African American male violence field. A blended perspective captures the essential elements for responding to partner abuse among African American men. In addition, programs must assess their capacity to work with African American male clients (Williams and Becker, 1994). A common philosophy should include the following points.

MEN WHO BATTER MUST BE HELD ACCOUNTABLE FOR THEIR BEHAVIOR

Battering is a crime. Legal sanctions that confront men who batter must be enforced. Men who batter are 100 percent responsible for their violence. Group facilitators must be willing to inform the probation officer, court officer or employ legal consequences for men who don't view treatment as a privilege. Furthermore, they must inform women who are at risk from potential violence, particularly if the client appears to be a danger to himself or to the intimate partner. Among African Americans, community standards must be strong enough to protect women and to confront the men who batter (Williams, 1993).

Another important issue is creating access to treatment. Court-mandated or court-referred programs have expanded in recent years. In some communities they exist to the exclusion of voluntary programs. It is imperative that both court-mandated and voluntary community based programs are available. The legal system cannot be expected to identify and refer all men who are violent. Community efforts must encourage men to seek treatment for violent and abusive behavior without legal interventions.

THERE IS NO JUSTIFICATION FOR MALE VIOLENCE

Societal oppression, internalized racism, violent social learning environment, sexism and male socialization are some of the influences that may result in violence toward women. However, these explanations do not *justify* the behavior. The behavior is damaging to the victim and all those concerned. It must be emphasized that partner abuse is destructive to African American women, families and communities. Increasing awareness about the influences on negative behavior should encourage men to behave in balance. It is essential to find adaptive nondestructive responses to societal or environmental challenges. Treatment groups and healthy supporting environments should be vehicles for learning nonviolent strategies.

MEN WHO BATTER MUST LEARN ALTERNATIVES TO VIOLENCE

In conventional approaches to domestic violence treatment, men learn alternatives to violence. Group treatment facilitators explore the predisposing influences for and conflict situations that can result in violence toward women. The content of treatment for African American men who batter must expand to include the ways in which social oppression and social learning from hostile community environments may result in violence toward women. African American men who batter must examine their reactions to social oppression. They should examine their code of conduct and rules for living. These then must make the link between their own frustration and their displacement of that anger onto women. They also must gain skills for negotiating a stressful oppressive social context. Particular African American men who batter must learn the connection between violence among peers and the generalization of that violence to intimate partner relationships. Such men must develop skills to negotiate and reframe the rules he learned from his violent environments.

REDUCE SEXIST ATTITUDES AND BEHAVIOR

Sexism gives all men who batter a license to abuse. This is a common phrase in the field and is as true for African American men as for any other racial or cultural group. Although African American men (and men from other cultures) are sometimes abusive in interracial relationships, the vast majority of male-female relationships between African Americans are intraracial. The dynamics around feminism, sexism and power between African American women and men differ in several aspects compared to White women and men (Hooks, 1995 and Staples, 1982). African American men must be confronted about their own specific brand of sexism, rather than using the models for White-male-female relationships (Staples, 1982). Clearly, power and control are a part of the manifestation of sexism, but history, circumstances and role expectations contribute. What is similar throughout definitions of sexism is that women are expected to be in the subordinate position.

SOCIAL OPPRESSION, SEXISM
AND AFRICAN AMERICAN WOMEN

African American women's history with sexism, past and present, has been shaped by the African American woman's experiences and realities with social oppression in the United States. If a counselor describes these dynamics from a Euro-American perspective, African American men may question its relevance. Williams (1993) made several observations while conducting presentations on domestic violence and sexism among African American audiences. Oppenlander (1981) traced what is identified as the history of partner abuse. We learn that it can be traced back to the Holy Roman Empire through Europe, England and to the United States. The legal codes that gave men permission to dominate, control and abuse women have been traced as well. Although this history is important and true, frequently when I recite such information in presentation or in counseling, many African American men and women have asked the following questions:

- What does that history have to do with me? Our Ancestors didn't come through Europe; they came through Africa. Accordingly, although battering is similar, Anglo history neither has the same relevance and importance to our experience, nor does it contribute to our understanding of ourselves.
- How did the violence of slavery influence domestic violence in partner relationships? That is, African American women were victimized, beaten and raped as slaves by their White slave holders. Why is that never mentioned in the history of domestic violence? What happened in their partner relationships?

- Was there no empathy concerning the African American woman's plight, or was the male slave partner equally as destructive as the master?

- Did the slave community have an impact on the sexism of African American women or on ending the violence?

- How was partner abuse and sexism shaped by African Americans after slavery?

- Weren't African American women still at high risk for abuse by Whites after slavery? Were they abused by partners too?

- How was partner abuse experienced by free Blacks in the North?

- How were African American women included in these legal codes which denied women rights? Said differently, legal codes in our nation's history have often been hostile toward us as a African people. Were African American women and White American women treated the same? Were legal codes equally antagonistic to White women?

- History demonstrates that White women, as well as African American women and men, have been disenfranchised by laws. How have such race and gender interactions shaped the experiences of domestic violence pertaining to African Americans?

- What role did African American women, men, the African American community and the Black Church play in ending violence against women?

- What is our history; what is our perspective; and what can we learn from this to help end and heal the problem?

Oppenlander's women's history of partner abuse is in fact a White history of partner abuse. I am convinced that addressing the differences regarding partner abuse is helpful for the African American community. Such information provides historical relevance, promotes ownership of the problem, and may explain the range of issues we must address within our context—just as it has done for White Americans.

SCAPEGOATED AFRICAN AMERICAN WOMEN

Battered African American women report that their partner attributes their violence to experiences with racism and oppression in society. African American men who batter must consider that if social oppression influences their life, African American women are affected by that same oppression. In fact, African American women experience a double oppression: societal oppression, and the oppression of sexism and partner abuse. Violence toward African American women may be a form of displaced frustration; however, she is being scapegoated because of *his* frustrations. If an African American man who batters, is mindful of the oppression he experiences, he must also be mindful of the oppression she does (Williams, 1994).

Richie (1995) in her gender entrapment theory encourages us to examine what families, particularly African American families, do to deny sexism and abusive behavior to women in order to protect male perpetrators. African American women know that the men's oppression is real. Moreover, Asbury (1989) describes the double-bind many African American women and families face—being concerned about how their men will be treated in a legal system that historically has been unjust. At the same time, they hate being victimized by his violence. So, often, women endure these hostile, violent, relationships to support their partner (or family member) in order to keep the family together, or because she believes she can heal him and/or he will change. For safety's sake, African American battered women must not accept this rationale as a reason to stay with someone who is out of control. She must be informed that she is at risk for violence if she stays or if she leaves. She cannot heal his pain through loyalty because he must heal himself. Men who batter are 100 percent responsible for their behavior. African American men who batter must be confronted on this issue and be reminded that African American women are faced with social oppression, too.

HEALING AND RESTORATION

In the United States, the standard for masculinity is based on a EuroAmerican model and has its origins in a capitalist economic and social order that emphasizes power, domination, independence, individualism, competitiveness and inexpressiveness (Pleck & Pleck, 1980; Roberts, 1994). African American men may feel the need to adopt a such a definition of masculinity that has been described as white male oriented, protective, guarded, competitive, condescending, patriarchal, dominant, aggressive and often violent—particularly with respect to women (Blake and Darling 1994; Franklin, 1984; Roberts, 1994).

Roberts (1994) asserts that it is assumed that African American men's positive ways of relating to women can contribute to an understanding of men's realities and possibilities. Furthermore, rarely is the public (and certain African American males) exposed to African American men as playing more positive roles in healthy and constructive relationships: as models, non-violent parents, providers, workers, partners and husbands (Blake and

Darling, 1994; Hare and Hare, 1984; Staples, 1986). But these positive behaviors and images are realities among African American men, as well.

The idea of healing and restoration is based on the reality that there are powerful positive models of African American manhood that all African American men must strive toward. Havenaar (1990) states that psychotherapy models can provide healing if they are based on the morals, cultural values and realities of a client group. He notes that every culture has its own Menschanschauung (set of cultural values) that is used to resocialize and heal its people. Unless African American men have healthy definitions of manhood, based on what can be described as an African American set of values, problems will occur (Akbar, 1989; Asanti, 1981; Madhubuti, 1984; and Roberts, 1994). Hooks (1995) and Roberts (1988) state that African American men must define themselves based on a healthy definition of masculinity, rather than based on a destructive, sexist or borrowed definition. Hooks (1994) reminds African American men not to recreate the power and control paradigm that scapegoats and oppresses women. She reminds us that oppression is destruction to everyone. Roberts (1994) reports that when African American men adopt or recreate negative definitions of masculinity, they are embracing Euro-American symbols of masculinity that define male and female as mutually-exclusive components. African American men, in contrast, historically have valued African American women as assertive, independent and competent, and have embraced a duality of role identity for women and men. Asanti (1981), Akbar (1985), and Roberts (1994) describe a set of enduring values that characterize African Americans. These include the importance of group and community above competition and individual aspirations. Furthermore, sharing, respect and reciprocity are valued in interpersonal relationships. Makubiti (1984) suggests in a poem entitled, "Black Manhood: Toward a Definition," that an African American man must live a life of balance. Akbar (1989) expands on this theme and encourages African Americans to live in balance within a community of self and others. Waldram (1994) suggests that for one to attain balance and healing he/she must actively focus on behaviors and action steps. To transform African American men who batter, these men must have accurate information about their history as healthy (non-dysfunctional, non-pathological) people. They must meet and interact with healthy models. Men who batter must be taught the rules for African American male health, which include: living in balance, learning how to negotiate life's challenges adaptively and without violence, and being respectful and inclusive of African American women and children. Finally, as they follow the action steps, they must strive to become models themselves.

SUMMARY

An enriched perspective retains the beliefs presently held in the field of partner abuse, but it differs because African American male perspectives are included as ingredients that shape the treatment content and design. For example, there is no justification for partner abuse; men who batter must take responsibility and be held accountable for their behavior; violent men must learn alternatives to violence, and controlling, sexist attitudes and behaviors. Accordingly, culturally competent programs will also include traditional and alternative explanations for violence among African American men who batter in approaches to treatment. Treatment interventions must incorporate these explanations and make the link between these explanations and his behavior. Violent African American men must learn how to negotiate life challenges due to social context and environment. In domestic violence treatment groups and in the African American community, it is essential to address healing, identity and community responsibility.

Engaging and confronting African American men who batter requires the capacity to respond to dual realities of those of battered women and African American men who batter. First and foremost, we must protect women from abuse. We must also develop a language to talk about alternative perspectives to confronting domestic violence. We must expand the present perception for the causes and solutions of violence. We must enrich present methods of treatment to be more inclusive: A one-size-fits-all approach is not always appropriate. Scholars and practitioners who study African Americans and those in the domestic violence community must talk to each other, work with each other and learn from each other. Finally, African Americans are caught in a peculiar predicament. Racism and oppression shape their experiences, perceptions and interactions in profound ways that continue to endure. Some survive oppression better than others. Those who don't may turn against themselves through destructive responses to self, to those they profess to love and to the community. Such destructive behavior can be seen as another tool of racism—internalized oppression. For some African American men, violence may be due to sexism, internalized oppression and displaced anger; for others, it is male socialization and control. There must be legal sanctions to protect women from abuse but there must also exist community sanctions appropriated by African Americans, which protect women and confront men who batter. Violence erodes a community's capacity to care for itself. At a recent speech at the University of Minnesota, Dr. Robert Allen, the author of *Black Awakenings* and co-author of *Brotherman*, made the following comments regarding domestic violence and African American men:

African American men know intimately the violent capabilities of other men. It is a tragedy that some of us have internalized the violence of this racist/sexist society and brought it into our communities and our homes. The injuries done by racism to black men's bodies and spirits are sometimes devastating, but this can never justify transforming that hurt into rage and violence against black women's bodies and spirits. We may not yet be able to stop the violence of the racist state, but self-inflicted violence in our communities and homes we can stop. Black men, who well know the lash of white male violence, have a special responsibility to stand with black women and children against all forms of violence. Black men must hold each other responsible for challenging sexism in our community as we all challenge the racism of white America . . . at the million man march, disavowing wife abuse, abuse of children, and the use of misogynist language was an affirming and healing gesture.

The domestic violence field and the community of African Americans must collaborate in affirming and healing gestures to reduce this problem in this community. To end this problem in all African American, White, Latino, Asian, and Native American communities. We must value our similar and unique realities with this problem and support our communities recovery efforts.

REFERENCES

Akabar, N. (1985). Our destiny: Authors of scientific revolution. In H. P. McAdoo & J. L. McAdoo (Eds.), *Black children: Social educational, and parental environments.* Beverly Hills, CA: Sage.

Asante, M. (1981). Black male and female relationships: An Afrocentric context. In L. Gary (Eds.), *Black men.* Beverly Hills, CA: Sage.

Bandura, A., Ross, D., & Ross, S. A. (1963). A comparative test of status envy, social power, and secondary reinforcement theories of identificatory learning. *Journal of Abnormal and Social Psychology, 67,* 527–534.

Bell, Y. R., Bouie, C. L., & Baldwin, J. A. (1990). Afrocentric cultural consciousness and African-American male-female relationships. *Journal of Black Studies,* 21(2), 162–189.

Berkowitz, L. (1983). The goals of aggression. In D. Finkelhor (Ed.), *The dark side of families.* Beverly Hills, CA: Sage.

Blake, W. M., & Darling, C. A. (1994). The dilemmas of the African American male. *Journal of Black Studies,* 24(4), 402–415.

Chestang, L. W. (1976). *Environmental influences on social functioning: The Black experience,* in P. Cafferty & L. Chestang (Eds.), *The diverse society: Implications for social policy,* Association Press: New York.

Cicone, M., & Ruble, D. (1978). Belief about males. *Journal of Social Issues, 34*(1), 5–15.

Edleson, J. L. (1984). Working with men who batter. *Social Work* (May/June), 237–241.

Edleson, J. L. & Eisikovits (Eds.) (1996). *Future interventions with battered women and their families.* Beverly Hills, CA: Sage Publications.

Ellis, T. (1995). What does it feel like to be a problem? In D. Belton (Ed.), *Speak my name: Black men on masculinity and the American Dream.*

Gary, L. E. (1995). African American men's perceptions of racial discrimination: A sociocultural analysis. *Social Work Research 19*(4), 207–217.

Gibbs, J. (1988). *Young, Black, and male: An endangered species.* Dove, MA: Auburn.

Gondolf, E. W. (1988). Who are those guys? Toward a behavioral typology of batterers. *Violence and Victims, 3,* 187–203.

Gondolf, E. W. (1985). *Men Who Batter: An Integrated Approach for Stopping Wife Abuse.* Learning Publications Inc.

Havenaar, J. M. (1990). Psychotherapy: Healing by culture. *Psychotherapy & Psychosomatics, 53*(1–4), 8–13.

Hammond, R. W., & Yung, B. (1993). Psychology's role in the public health response to assaultive violence among young African American men. *American Psychologist, 48*(2), 142–154.

Hawkins, D. F. (1987). Devalued lives and racial stereotypes: Ideological barriers to the prevention of family violence among blacks. In R. L. Hampton (Ed.). *Violence in the Black family: Correlates and consequences,* Lexington, MA: Lexington Books.

Holtzworth-Munroe, A., & Stuart, G. (1994). Typologies of male batterers: Three subtypes and the differences among them. *Psychological Bulletin, 116*(3), 476–497.

Hooks, B. (1994). *Outlaw culture: Resisting representations.* New York: Routledge.

Hooks, B. (1995). *Killing rage: Ending racism.* NY: Owl Books.

Lemelle, A. J. (1995a). *Black male deviance.* Westport, CT: Prager.

Lemelle, A. J. (1995). The Political Sociology of Black Masculinity and Tropes of Domination. *Journal of African American Men, 1*(2), 87–101.

Madhubuti, H. R. (1984). *Earthquakes and sun rise missions: Poetry and essays of Black renewal 1973–1983.* Chicago: Third World Press.

Madhubuti, H. R. (1990). *Black men obsolete, single, dangerous? The Afrikan family in transition.* Chicago: Third World Press.

McCall, N. (1994). *Makes me wanna holler: A young Black man in America.* New York: Random House.

Nicholson, D. (1995). On violence. In Belton, D. (Ed.) *Speak my name: Black men on masculinity and the American dream.* Boston: Beacon Press.

Norton, D. (1978). The dual perspective. In *The Dual Perspective: Inclusion of Ethnic Minority Content in Social Work Curriculum.* New York: Council on Social Work Education.

Oliver, W. (1994). *The violent social world of African American men.* New York: Lexington Books.

Oppendlander, N. (1981). The evolution of law and wife abuse. *Law and Policy Quarterly, 3*(4), 382–405.

Peled, E. (1996). Secondary victims no more: Refocusing interventions with children. In J. L. Edleson & Eisikovits (Eds.), *Future interventions with battered women and their families.* CA: Sage Publications.

Pence, E. (1989). Batterer programs: Shifting from community collusion to community confrontation. In P. L. Casear & L. K. Hamberger (Eds.), *Treating men who batter: Theory, practice, and programs.* New York: Springer.

Pleck, J., & Pleck, E. (1980). *The American man.* Englewood Cliffs, NJ: Prentice-Hall.

Rich, J. A., & Stone, D. A. (1996). The experience of violent injury for young African American men: The meaning of being a sucker, *Journal of General Internal Medicine, 11*, 77–82.

Richie, B. (1995). Gender entrapment: when battered women are compelled to crime. (*Proceedings of the National Institute on Domestic Violence in the African American Community*.) U.S. Department of Health and Human Services. Administration for Children and Families. Office of Community Services.

Roberts, G. W. (1994). Brother to brother: African American modes of relating among men, *Journal of Black Studies, 24*(4), 379–390.

Rothenberg, P. S. (1988). *Racism and sexism: An integrated study*. New York: St. Martin's.

Rosenberg, M. (1990). Change to participants: From analysis to action. *Public Health Reports, 106*, 233–235.

Rosenberg, M., & Mercy, J. (1991). Assaultive violence. In M. Roesenberg & J. Mercy (Eds.), *Violence in America: A public health approach*. New York: Oxford University Press.

Roy, M. (Ed.), (1982). *The abusive partner: An analysis of domestic battering*. New York: Van Nostrand Reinhold.

Saunders, D. G. (1992). A typology of men who batter women: Three types derived from cluster analysis. *American Orthopsychiatry, 62*, 264–275.

Saunders, D. G., & Parker, J. C. (1989). Legal sanctions and treatment follow through among men who batter: A multivariate analysis. *Social Work Research and Abstracts, 25*(3), 21–29.

Sonkin, D. J., Martin, D., & Walker, L. E. (1985). *The male batterer: A treatment approach*. New York: Springer Publishing.

Straus, M. (1980). Victims and aggressor in marital violence. *American Behavioral Scientist, 23*(5), 681–704.

Tolman, R. T, & Bennett, L. (1990). A review of quantitative research on men who batter. *Journal of Interpersonal Violence, 5*(1) 87–118.

Waldram, J. B. (1993). Aboriginal spirituality: Symbolic healing in Canadian prisons. *Culture, Medicine & Psychiatry, 17*(3), 345–362.

Westra, B., & Martin, H. (1980). Children of battered women. *Maternal and Child Nursing*, 41–53.

Williams, O. J., & Becker, L. R. (1994). Domestic partner abuse treatment programs and cultural competence: The results of a national study. *Violence and Victims, 8*(3), 287–296.

Williams, O. J. (1994). Group work with African American men who batter: Toward more ethnically-sensitive practice. *Journal of Comparative Family Studies, 25*(1), 91–103.

Williams, O. J. (1994). Treatment for African American men who batter, *Cura Reporter, 25*(3), 6–10.

Williams, O. J. (1993). Developing an African American perspective to reduce spouse abuse: Considerations for community action. *Black Caucus: Journal of the National Association of Black Social Workers, 1*(2), 1–8.

Williams, O. J. (1992). Ethnically sensitive practice in enhancing the participation of the African American man who batters. *Families in Society: The Journal of Contemporary Human Services, 73*(10), 588–595.

Williams, O. J., & Griffin. L. W. (1991). Elder abuse in the Black family. In R. L. Hampton (Ed.), *Black family violence: Current research and theory* (pp. 117–127). Lexington, MA: Lexington Books.

Williams, O. J. (1990). Spouse abuse: Social learning, attribution and interventions. *Journal of Health and Social Policy, 1*(2), 91–109.

Williams, O. J. (in press). Working in groups with African American men who batter. In L. D. Davis (Ed.), *A guide to working with African American men.* Newbury Park, CA: Sage Publications.

Wilson, A. N. (1992). *Understanding Black adolescent male violence: Its remediation and prevention.* New York: Afrikan World InfoSystems.

Yllo, K. & Bogard, M. (Eds.) (1988). *Feminist perspectives on wife abuse.* Newbury Park, CA: Sage.

5

A Postcolonial Perspective on Domestic Violence in Indian Country

Eduardo Duran, Bonnie Duran,
Wilbur Woodis, and Pamela Woodis

DREAM*

I was sitting on a hill overlooking a river, and in the distance I could tell I was sitting on the north side of the river. Looking to my left, I could see that was the east, south was straight ahead of me, to my right was the west, and behind me was the north.

I was sitting there watching things—the clouds, the wind blowing, the river down below—and all of a sudden the earth started shaking and everything just started moving. Clouds rolled in, and there was thunder and lightning. It was really interesting because everything was shaking and things were noisy. It was getting darker and darker. Then I realized I kind of saw something making a movement to my left. I looked and the place I was sitting turned into a bunch of kivas (Anasazi ceremonial structures, partly underground). I looked and there were people popping out of the ground, jumping from the kivas. They were actually running toward me, and past me, up to the highest point of the hill. So I got up and joined everybody else on this plateau area. It was still dark and stormy, and all kinds of people were there. All of a sudden, out of the sky came a yucca plant. It was really long, and the tip of it was on fire. As soon as it hit the ground, everything stopped. There was just complete silence.

---

*By Wilbur Woodis

I looked down and saw the tip of the yucca burning and went to pick it up. As I bent down to touch it, a voice said, "Don't touch that." So I backed away, and in just a few seconds there was a couple of Pygmy-like people coming from the south over the hill. They were painted in shades of greens and reds. There were two of them, and they both had an evergreen plant or a tip of a young piñon in their hands. They came running and then just stopped. They seemed like they were having fun, really. So they walked around and they were speaking their own language. This was interesting, because I could understand them. What they asked everyone was, "Did anyone touch that thing that fell out of the sky?" And everyone pointed at me and said, "He did." Of course, I hadn't, but they came over and started hitting me all over my body with the tops of the young trees. Then they did the same to everyone else that was on top of the hill. It was still dark and they continued the ritual. They seemed sort of hyper as they finished, then they went to the west, back over the hill, and disappeared.

As soon as they disappeared, a man appeared on the right side, from the north. He had a cape on, and a long staff, and I know he had braids. The yucca was still on the ground, smoldering, and the fire wasn't that big. But the man grabbed the burning yucca and put it in his cape. Then he left and went back in the same direction he came from.

As I was standing around and thinking this was kind of strange, all of a sudden I could hear this lady's voice screaming behind me, which was a little to the northwest, "Help me!"

I turned around and walked a little way down the hill, and there was this cage sitting on the side of one of the kivas. Inside of it was a woman, so I walked over there. I could hear people yelling and screaming behind me, and could hear them saying, "Don't let her out! She's crazy! Don't let her out!" I didn't really listen to them and before I realized what I was doing, I opened the cage. As soon as I did that, the sun rose and the sky cleared. Then I woke up from my dream.

INTRODUCTION

During recent years there have been many attempts to understand domestic violence in our society. Many intervention and research projects have been launched that would shed some light on the problem. It is well known that violence continues to grow, and many people fear that they may become a victim of violence. Although there has been an attempt to examine domestic violence in this society, it is remarkable that very few studies have been conducted in Indian country. Presently, we do not know the extent of domestic violence in Indian communities since no comprehensive epidemiological studies exist.

Through the collective clinical and community work that the authors have been doing over the past 20 years, it is safe to say that there is at least as much domestic violence in Indian country as there is in the rest of society. At any rate, there are no data to disprove the authors' findings. The fact that the problem is almost completely ignored by researchers and funders of research is an indictment of a social science system that chooses to further the violence by ignoring it.

Many of the models for treatment are based on Western interventions. Imposing these models of intervention on Indian people would merely perpetrate another form of violence and further colonization on our community. Epistemic violence[1] of this sort may be one of the contributing factors to the high rate of violence in Indian country. Therefore, the authors will take a different road in the analysis of and treatment recommendations for domestic violence in Indian country.

Theories that have emerged on domestic violence do not exist in a vacuum and they may be ladened with attempts at social control of Indian peoples.

> Recent philosophical and scientific advances counsel us that theories do not mirror or correspond to reality; at best they are tools. This realization opens up space for investigation into not what is but what works. . . . These approaches, however useful, are not neutral insights and assessments of native drinking patterns but rather venture to explain and predict behavior based on a very historically and culturally specific mode of representation—realism—which erroneously assumes unity between the sensible and intelligible. Embedded within this Eurocentric mode of representation is a biased assessment of non-Western cultures. Behavioral theories decontextualize and individualize social problems and many sociocultural theories continue European representations of native peoples that have origins in the politics of the colonial and early American era. Insofar as these approaches are cultural products—a form of literature—we can say that they are hegemonic. By this we mean that they partake in ideological/cultural domination by the assertion of universality and neutrality and by the disavowal of all other cultural forms or interpretations. (Duran & Duran, 1995, p. 110)

Academics and clinicians believe that alcohol may be the most significant contributing factor to domestic violence. This type of thinking is simplistic and fails to place the problem in the proper context. Alcohol may be

---

[1]Epistemic violence occurs when production of meaning and knowledge fails to capture the truth of Native and tribal lives. For a further discussion, refer to Spivak (1988).

closely related to the problems underlying domestic violence thus being more parallel than hierarchical in relationship. "A review of the existing literature on the subject of Native Americans and alcohol contains gross inconsistencies between what is considered by many to be the genesis of the problem and suggestions for its amelioration. In addition, all but a few authors maintain a definition of the problem that masks the issues of domination and subjugation, issues which must be considered given the historical context of this problem" (Duran & Duran, 1995, p. 106).

Hegemonic discourse through the propagation of psychological literature posing as neutral because of its Eurocentric scientism has been violent toward Indian people, and presently this violence has targeted Indian men. Many of the approaches that pretend to heal the pain of domestic violence instead seek someone to victimize and blame. Workshops and other methods of disseminating information on the topic single out men in the community and label them pathological without any consideration for historical context. The most simplistic empirical question may be "How much domestic violence was there before White contact?" From all the oral accounts that we have, it is safe to say that the Indian males in precolonial times had a much more nurturing and respected role in the community.

We are not advocating romanticized remembering of the past. Even without the devastation of colonialism, there would have been changes within Native American structures and systems over time. However, those changes would have taken place within the context of cultural change and development. In addition, in the precolombian world there were systemic structures to deal with family and community problems. These healing systems were systematically destroyed throughout the colonization process. We discuss here some of the subjugated knowledge of the events that led to the present world of Native Americans and their families. In the process we hope to provide space for reimagining the present. This reimagining is also an important component of the treatment process.

We realize that not all tribes or all Native American people were subjected to the same amount of trauma. The discussion here is to illustrate the effects of trauma on the tribes and people who suffered as colonization occurred. The problems that our communities face today are a result, at least in part, of not being given the time and resources to resolve the trauma. A belief by some that present symptomology is merely because the Native American community is deficient in one way or another is a form of epistemic violence that only exacerbates the problem. It is especially sad to see that epistemic violence is being utilized by some Indian people working within institutions that supposedly are there to help Indian people.

RELEVANT DATA

Unfortunately very little data is available on Native Americans and domestic violence. A study was done that presents some data on violence in Indian country. Bachman (1992) found that there is an estimated 37,000 assaults on Indians per year. Violent incidents between husband and wife occur at the rate of 15.5% versus 14.8% for White couples. Severe violence by husbands occurs at the rate of 12.2% versus 11.0% for White couples. The authors find that "it can be seen that the American Indian rate of couple violence is 5 percent higher than the White rate. When this is limited to severe violence, American Indian families experience nearly 36 percent more assaultive behaviors than do White families. Similarly, when husband-to-wife violence is compared, any violence perpetrated by husbands is about 10 percent higher in American Indian families, and severe violence by American Indian husbands is 6 percent higher" (Bachman, 1992, p. 104). The authors caution that these rates are "lower bound" estimates due to sampling problems when researching American Indians.

Results from the study are tentative. Understanding about Indian families continues to be fragmented, anecdotal, descriptive, and overpowered by poor understanding and inadequate research methodologies. Bachman (1992) recommended: "With regard to domestic violence, future research should focus on exploring such violence within more homogeneous units, such as specific tribal and reservation communities. Urban and rural differences also need to be considered. American Indian intrafamily violence is a complex and multifaceted issue" (p. 107).

THEORETICAL BACKGROUND

It is unreasonable to begin understanding health related problems in Indian country without first realizing that the genesis of many of the factors related to the problems are historical in nature. Central to the historical contribution to the problem of domestic violence is the factor of historical trauma. In addition to historical trauma being a critical variable we must then examine how internalized oppression contributes to the suffering of Indian families.

Recent literature clearly demonstrates how historical trauma continues to manifest itself in all types of unhealthy behavior patterns across Indian country (Braveheart-Jordan & DeBruyn, 1995; Duran & Duran, 1995). Briefly stated, historical trauma is unresolved trauma and grief that continues to adversely affect the lives of survivors of such trauma. It is remarkable that historical trauma is passed from one generation to the next and is also cumulative. Therefore, the pain and suffering inflicted on Indian people several generations ago can contribute to the suffering that occurs today.

Internalized oppression is a factor because it is pain that is not resolved and instead is projected onto someone close to the person who has suffered personal or historical trauma. The notion of internalized oppression illustrates how pain that the person carries, if not resolved, may be imposed on someone else. The incidence of domestic violence provides evidence indicating that there is significant unresolved trauma in the Indian community.

Within the internalized oppression paradigm, male dynamics have a specific expression. "The Lakota wicasa, or man, was robbed of his traditional role as hunter, protector (warrior) and provider. He lost status and honor. This negatively impacted his relationship with Lakota women and children. A further assault on the Lakota and all Indian peoples was the prohibition against indigenous spiritual practices in 1883" (Braveheart-Jordan & DeBryun, 1995, p. 351). The removal of roles for men affected the societal system, thus paving the way for unhealthy family patterns of behavior. Without access to spiritual ceremony, Indian people were susceptible to other forms of spiritual colonization and hegemony. The emptiness caused by cultural genocide left the people open to a foreign cosmological way of being.

European cosmology has been heavily influenced by Judeo-Christian thought. Core to this cosmology is the concept that everything is in opposition or in an antagonistic relationship. This antagonistic relationship is further compounded by the fact that there has been a subject—object split in the Western psyche. Western thinking is therefore prone to seeing the world as separate and something to be dominated (in Genesis, God tells Adam that everything is in His charge and He is dominant over the earth). This perspective has been responsible for the colonization of native peoples.

Thinking based on antagonism plays a significant part in human relationships. In Western thinking, Feminine and Masculine naturally are in opposition rather than existing harmoniously. If Feminine and Masculine are in opposition to each other, it makes sense that strife rather than peace and harmony is a more predictable way of relating. Antagonistic psychology is not the only way of being in the lifeworld, and there are many indigenous peoples who perceive the world in a completely different fashion.

We will be using a framework that is part of the Dine' (Navajo)[2] traditional worldview to describe harmonious relationships. We will

---

[2]By using Dine' cosmology we do not intend to say that this is the only way to understand the dynamics. Other tribes can analyze the dynamics through a similar process utilizing their own tribally specific stories. What we attempt to offer here is a method of analysis, i.e. process instead of content.

demonstrate how domestic violence may have some of its deep roots in a cosmology of antagonism. We will discuss how the clinical process can facilitate understanding in the client which will in turn enable the client to lead a more harmonious life with people from another gender (this sentence was difficult to write because the usual way of saying this would be "lead a more harmonious life with the opposite sex").

SLAYER OF MONSTERS AND CHILD BORN OF WATER

One must be careful and respectful when introducing oral teaching related to lifeways of the native peoples. At times it is difficult presenting native words using the English language, therefore, graphic representations have been provided to reinforce theoretical discussions.

The oral teachings of the Navajo people accompanied by parallel concepts of their Athapaskan cousins, the Apaches, will be used to illustrate knowledge that can help young men and women learn to respect self-growth, marriage, family, tribe, and community. In setting the stage for teaching purposes, it must be made clear that there are many versions of the cosmic/mystical/soulful/spiritual relationship between man and woman. Life-giving forces as taught by the Navajo, Apache, and other indigenous peoples are complex and require an immersion into that life-world. What follows can be described as a mere paraphrasing of sacred knowledge to bring about what Western psychology describes as a cognitive shift in understanding accompanied by discourse hopefully leading to new paradigms. These new insights can help a human being see other perspectives and understand how self-hate (the spirit of internalized oppression) can be controlling his or her life and causing imbalance. It is hoped that this ancient model of knowledge will help our brothers and sisters explore paths of self-healing practiced for centuries by our predecessors. Some believe that this knowledge has been forgotten. We believe it is still alive, just as our mother earth continues to provide us with gifts of growth as she relates with father sky.

Figure 5.1 depicts the universal concept of duality between male and female. In the Dine' (Navajo) cosmology, the soul (psyche) of the male and female lies within each person regardless of sex. The female side is called Tobajishchini (child born of water), and the male side is Naayeeneizghani (slayer of monsters). The paternal father for both of these children is Johonaaei (sun or fire), and the maternal mother is Asdaanadleei (changing woman) for slayer of monsters and Yoolgaiasdzaa (white shell woman) for child born of water. Changing woman is identified as White Painted Woman by the Jicarilla Apache (Opler, 1938). Changing woman/white

FIGURE 5.1   Gender and power cosmology.

painted woman is related to the earth. White shell women is related to water. The last god or spirit is Nilchi (wind or air), who blew the breath of life into monster slayer and child born of water. One could interpret this story as a description of the birth of the human soul (this is closely related to the Judeo-Christian story of the creation of man, in which God blew the air of life into the molded clay). In the Navajo puberty ceremony the young female represents both changing woman and white shell woman. In the Jicarilla Apache puberty rite the female represents white shell woman and child born of water, and the young brave also represents child born of water (Opler, 1938). In the Navajo tradition the male appears to play a lesser role, and the female represents mother earth and all creation. Earth, air, fire, and water are a common theme among indigenous peoples and are glorified through worship.

Changing woman literally is changing constantly through the generations of people. In other words since our physical mother is made of earth and we are brought into life by the female, we are part of the female energy. The changes occur through our changing across the life cycle. At any one time there are old people and young people alive, representing all phases of the life cycle. Therefore, changing woman lives perpetually in all forms, changing yet constant. The myth is alive in every moment, with ancestors and unborn also being an integral part of the present moment.

Saa,ah'naagei can be described as sky/sun/moon/stars and beyond, and Beeke,hoozoon can be described as ground/earth/water, with the wind/air acting as mediator. What is not described is the interaction between earth and sky and how this relates to harmonious life and balance between and within men and women, as seen from the teachings of the Dine' culture. The interaction between the life force or center of sky, earth, and the four directions taken as a whole is the soul of man and woman which must be kept in balance by constant self-evaluation, prayer, and offerings to all life forces including the seventh sacred direction, which is the human being. This postcolonial[3] concept appears to run counter to the Western view of the relationship between the different genders.

(Figure 5.2, top) illustrates the western view of the relationship between man and woman. There appears to be a linear "tug of war" between the two sexes. The image depicting the yin and yang (Figure 5.2, bottom) represents the interrelationship of energies. Within this paradigm and cosmology the energies are not in antagonism; instead they coexist within each other. In Figure 5.2 (top) it is apparent that western male masculine-ism verses western female feminine-ism[4] creates tension between the sexes leading to struggles for power and control. Figure 5.2 (bottom) represents masculine and feminine existing within and through each other. The antagonism that exists in Figure 5.2 (top) is no longer there.[5] Historically, the indigenous peoples of North and South America were forced to conform to the ideals and teachings of their colonizers. During the colonizing process, the harmonious cosmology was wounded. The wound and pain continue to cloud the previous state of psychological balance and ability to see the world as a harmonious place.

Figure 5.3 (top) consists of a combination of Figures 5.1 and 5.2. One postcolonial view of human beings as holistic is distorted by the Western

---

[3]Postcolonial can also be thinking that existed in precolonial times. In essence it is a way of being in the world that attempts to understand the effects of colonization and through this reflection allows the person to free themselves from the problems imposed by colonization. In depth analysis has been done in this area by Duran & Duran, 1995 and Braveheart-Jordan, 1995.

[4]The terms masculinism and femininism are used here to depict the undifferentiated sides of the respective energies. Masculinism is an energy that can be destructive and is a force that interplays in domestic violence. Femininism is the undifferentiated destructive side of the female energy that also interplays in domestic violence relationships. In Jungian jargon, these would be the shadow side of the anima or animus.

[5]We use the Chinese image representing the tao to make this more accessible to our readers. The understanding of male and female forces in the taoist teachings are for all practical purposes the same as the teachings we are offering. The only difference is the types of metaphors and images used to carry the same archetypal idea.

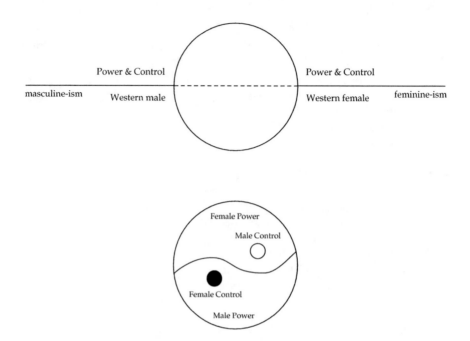

FIGURE 5.2   Gender and power in Western and Chinese cosmology.

view of human beings. The current body of knowledge being written about American Indians demonstrates how disease, captivity, violent death, starvation, forced relocation, and forced Western religious/academic education were the historical norm. Education of indigenous native children was carried out by rounding up children and moving them as far away from family, community, and land. This was done to ensure cultural hegemony of these children and their subsequent generations.

Even though many other attempts to acculturate and assimilate the indigenous natives of north America were made, traditional teachings survived. Most indigenous peoples have similar cosmologies about the relationship between male and female. These teachings may have been lost from consciousness but have remained as part of the personality and continue to emerge in dreams. Postcolonial psychology makes the case for indigenous knowledge having legitimacy and not allowing any other epistemology to be privileged over another. Indigenous healing ways continue to exist even at a time when "misoneism" predominates among contemporary Western psychological thought. Misoneism meaning fear, intolerance, and an oppressive hatred of new and innovative knowledge and an attitude of keeping these ancient healing teachings in the realm of a few.

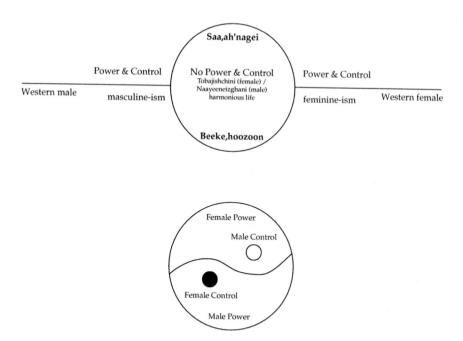

FIGURE 5.3   Model illustrating antagonistic relationships.

Figure 5.4 depicts the "spirit of the time" as related to issues of violence, specifically domestic violence. Western programming has forced indigenous people to follow the linear relationship between genders. The circle remains but is bypassed for a more Western form of domination. Postcolonial work begins by recognizing that both the circle and the line must become integrated or the violence will continue. A hybrid way of being in a bicultural lifeworld needs to develop in order to begin intervening in

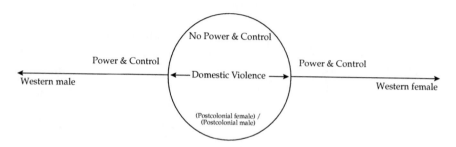

FIGURE 5.4   Linear relationship between genders.

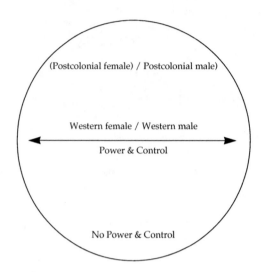

FIGURE 5.5   Healing of gender antagonism: Transitional phase.

domestic violence issues. Relating to the figure above, the line must be moved into the circle, but the circle cannot be moved into the line (see Figure 5.5). This process on the surface appears simple, but it is complex.

In essence, the problem becomes one of being able to conceptualize the world in a completely different way. This process cannot be forced, that is, the circle cannot be forced into the line (not without destroying its essence of circleness). We find that it is this very forceful process that is used in Western systems to make sense of different worldviews that do not fit a linear approach to the world.

For the integration process to begin current literature about indigenous people must be reevaluated through postcolonial analysis. This examination must be carried out by people with a vision of truly accepting indigenous knowledge as is. The attitude of the Western "A not B" versus the postcolonial "A:B" as presented by Duran & Duran (1995) should be integrated.[6] Briefly stated, this notion asserts that Indian identity should not be realized by comparing Indian people to what they are not, that is, non-White. Instead there should be distinct categories of identity that need no legitimization by another group.

------

[6]In many Western systems, people are identified by what they are not. We suggest that subjectivity be determined by what the person is. In other words, do not identify women as non-men. Instead, women should be identified as women.

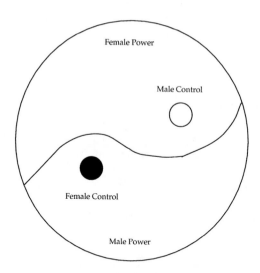

FIGURE 5.6 **Healing of gender antagonism: Balanced power.**

Literature continues to romanticize the indigenous American Indian experience of the past 500 years. Articles discuss the many different periods in history of subjugation of the natives, then immediately jump to blaming the victim, systematically overlooking the obvious. This form of epistemic violence is rarely discussed or acknowledged in most academic discussions and literature dealing with the psychology of indigenous peoples. Furthermore, many public health, social and clinical programs continue to go to battle in hopes of alleviating the indigenous psychosocial problems. Some of our own people have joined in this battle as well. Many of these programs are superficial in nature and powered by a Western frame of reference using monetary and academic tools of persuasion.

Integrating the linear thinkers of power and control with the circular cosmologies of indigenous peoples will serve to neutralize and reveal this power and control spirit (archetype). But first the historical dichotomy created within the indigenous psyche must be revealed. The dichotomy is this; I am a native man or woman who rides on this linear chair fueled by "power and control," and I have incorporated this line into my experience. Yet I am not fulfilled because this is not me, so I repress and dissociate these thoughts and feelings. At this point, respect between genders is forgotten and is replaced by Western ideas of power. I am an independent female who is discriminated against therefore I must create a movement against my oppressor, who is the male. On the other hand, the native Indian male simply accepts his stereotypical dominant role but has no power in the dominant or western society.

In prayer, the Jicarilla Apache and the Dine' will first sprinkle corn pollen on top of his or her head before it is sprinkled in the mouth and out to the external life forces as a gesture of respect and participation in any activity that serves to continue the legacy of the people and the person. The significance of this is that, in prayers, include "the person who stands inside me." If you are male, a female stands inside you; if you are female, a male stands inside you. In offering pollen in prayer in this manner, a balance in soul and a balance in nature are attained and maintained. This balancing ritual between the two life forces of male and female serves to remind both sides of the interrelationship and respect due each other.

The indigenous male finds himself attempting to be what he is not. In addition, his role is constantly being defined for him. According to Western thought he is a warrior, a shaman, and represents nature. He is a protector of our planet. If he does not meet these criteria, he is either assimilated and acculturated and has lost all remnants of his culture or he is a social problem who needs to be treated or locked up. It is understandable that one of the symptoms suffered by our men and women is that they try to destroy each other. The choices are limited and what remains is an individual who is forced to accept and live out either a romantic or tragic fantasy.

Postcolonial concepts of intervention bring to the surface these current definitions of what an Indian male should be. The use of interventions discussed in Duran and Duran (1995) can begin to provide clues to violence problems among native males without placing blame or forcing upon another teachings inconsistent with his or her worldview.

CLINICAL INTERVENTIONS

Some of the clinical interventions suggested in this section should be part of a full array of services offered to the individual or family. The strategies that we discuss focus on the cultural aspect of the intervention, and we assume that the providers have training and experience working in the area of domestic violence. The authors want to avoid the presentation of a therapy that may not be effective. At times clinicians who are not culturally competent take suggested approaches in a vacuum and neglect treating the case as a complete case.

A typical treatment protocol should address the following areas.

ASSESSMENT PHASE

The client must have a full assessment that will shed light on his overall functioning. Western-based assessment as well as assessment of cultural functioning must be performed. At this point, we will not elaborate on the Western functioning since such an assessment is well known and is described in other sections of this book.

Cultural assessment should follow a process that will yield cosmological information that is tribal specific. The analysis that we present here provides an example of how this may be done. By having the client understand his traditional cosmology, a template of health can be established. In other words, the client will know that violence and dysfunction are not a tribal way of life and that there is a different standard of behavior than the one he is accustomed to. Many times we have found that dysfunctional behavior has been in the family for so many generations that the client assumes that this is a traditional culturally sanctioned way to live.

THERAPEUTIC/HEALING PHASE

Once the client realizes that the dysfunction is a way of life imposed on a healthy traditional lifeworld, the therapy can begin to focus on the soul wound or historical trauma. It is our experience that by having the client understand the sociohistorical context, it becomes easier for him to let go of the guilt and anxiety that continue to grip him in the cycle of violence. The client can begin to understand how through the internalizing of trauma and the oppressor, he has acted out self destructive energy on his loved ones.

Therapy during this phase must take on a didactic approach. The therapist must be knowledgeable of the historical trauma and the effects that these events had on the Native American family structure. The clients must be made aware that a lot of the rage that he feels is internalized oppression and the violence a manifestation of that intergenerational spiritual injury.

At this point in the therapy the transference can move in two directions if the therapist is a Native American. If the therapist persists in working within the Western model, he or she will reinforce the internal oppressor that the client brings into treatment. Basically what the therapist is doing is disallowing either through ignorance or blind spot the historical reality that has brought the client into the session. It is highly recommended that these therapists undergo supervision or therapy so that they can resolve their own historical trauma. If therapy continues in this type of transference relationship it is merely recapitulating the dynamics of historical trauma. This will make for iatrogenic[7] results for both therapist and client. If the Native American therapist integrates the process of therapy through the reification of cultural ceremonial norms, the transference will develop towards the ceremony itself. At this point, it is the therapy or healing that is actually the object of projection.

With a Caucasian therapist, a different type of transference will be elicited. The client will project historical contents into the therapeutic ceremony. Caucasian therapists that we have worked or trained with usually have great difficulty with historical trauma issues. The guilt that is elicited by historical truth makes the guilt turn into anger; this anger in the therapeutic circle will result in failure and iatrogenic practice. Through acknowledgement of historical truth that validates the client's pain, therapy can become more successful. The therapist must take scrutiny and ownership of his or her history in order to have a more honest therapeutic encounter. In addition, the therapist must take responsibility for the way history has afforded him or her privilege in our current society. Without this honesty the therapy is bound to fail. Prevailing literature illustrates that most current Western therapeutic modalities with Native Americans are not very successful (Duran & Duran, 1995).

If the therapist understands historical trauma and brings this knowledge into the therapeutic ceremony, the transference becomes one of liberation. The client can see that the traditional cosmology is valid and is being lived out by one of the role models of the community in a bicultural, healthy manner. Through understanding and teaching of similar cosmology as presented here the client can free himself of the internal oppressor and start to resolve some of the personal issues that brought him into the healing circle in the first place. At this point, Western interventions can be made and the client can deal with the domestic violence that afflicts the family.

HYBRID THERAPY BROUGHT TO LIFE

A typical case would involve the therapist going through the teaching that is outlined in this chapter. The client would be made aware of the universality of the concept of male and female energy existing in everyone. The ideas of child born of water and slayer of monsters would be discussed in a way that the client will integrate the teaching into his present life. (Notions of anima and animus as described by Jung may be helpful for training therapists and helping them make sense of the traditional teaching.)

---

[7]Literally this means that the doctor is making the patient sick. For an in-depth study on this topic, read *The Iatrogenics Handbook* (Morgan, 1983).

The client should also be encouraged to record his dreams and to work on these images through a medium with which he is comfortable (i.e., painting, poetry, sandtray).

The clients can then be taught about the harmonious relationship that has existed between female and male energy throughout time. The tension between the energies is caused by a foreign interpretation of the relationship and the incorporation of a mythology that views relationships in cosmology as antagonistic. Once the antagonistic way of seeing the world is integrated, the personal myth is thrown into a chaotic unbalance. The anxiety created by the unbalance creates a power and control struggle between the male and female energy.

Historical trauma further complicates the overall picture through the internalizing of the oppressive energy, this energy has been mostly masculine energy.[8] This logocentric masculine energy is attracted to the masculine energy of the indigenous male. It is as if the logocentric energy is seeking a different form of balance that is more earth related. Because of historical trauma the indigenous male cannot assimilate the logocentric energy in a healthy, balanced way, and it becomes undifferentiated within his psyche. It is this undifferentiated energy that seeks to control and overpower the female energy and is manifested in violence.

The indigenous female has an energy that is qualitatively different in mythological makeup than the European energy. This energy can not harmonize with the undifferentiated logocentric energy that has taken over the male. Her balance and harmony are also placed in a chaotic situation, thus making her react in a manner that seeks to control in an antagonistic way. This chaotic unbalance provides the raw materials for antagonism and violence. Healing can occur only through a proper understanding of the dynamics that occur at a deep psychological and spiritual level.

There are times when the therapy can only go so far, even if the dynamics of this brief chapter are implemented. At this time it is imperative that the therapy incorporate ceremony through the consultation of traditional indigenous healers.[9] Within traditional ceremony it is possible to bring the spiritual energy back into balance. The ceremony must be used

---

[8]It is well known that Western mythology is based on the logocentric masculine principle. The logocentric energy has been behind much of the devastation of indigenous peoples as described in the historical trauma paradigm. These notions are discussed at length in Native American Post Colonial Psychology (Duran & Duran, 1995).

[9]Ceremonies are process oriented as the reader well knows. Therefore, it is not appropriate to give particulars on the type of ceremony used in the therapy since every healer has their own way of doing so. Therapists that need to incorporate this type of intervention must call qualified providers of such services in order to provide for the Native clients' needs.

within a model that employs some form of psychotherapy in order to help the client assimilate the healing in a way that makes some cognitive sense. Most of the medicine people we have worked with agree that the ceremony will take care of the spiritual component. Psychotherapy can help the client assimilate the process of the ceremony. Traditional healers prescribe methods of living that will help clients maintain the harmony achieved through ceremony, and the client has the responsibility to live and behave in a prescribed manner that will not create the chaos that afflicted him in the first place. At this point the therapist must be skilled and knowledgeable in traditional practices. The client can then be helped to bridge the continuum between ceremony and the daily lifeworld.

The reason it is so critical that the client be able to bridge between ceremony and lifeworld is that colonization has inflicted a wound in this area also. Western cosmology allows for the compartmentalization of the different aspects of the personality. Indian people have internalized the shadow side of compartmentalization, and some (the ones who are dysfunctional) find no connection between ceremony and daily life. Clients in this situation are searching for magical cures out of the ceremony and feel that they do not have responsibilities to live in a certain prescribed fashion outside of the ceremony proper. The compartmentalization has become so deep that many of our relatives have adopted the ceremony of chemical abuse and incorporated it into the daily lifeworld.

Figures 5.5 and 5.6 represent the restoration of the harmony between the different energies. The male and female who overcomes the effects of colonialism have moved into a postcolonial lifeworld. Figure 5.5 is the transitional phase where power and control enter into the circular paradigm. Through both traditional and western intervention the energy becomes harmonious as in Figure 5.6. Figure 5.6 represents aspects of both power and control from both male and female energy. Since the energy is in balance, there is no antagonism that can be acted out, as is seen in cases of domestic violence. At this point, the ceremony is complete.

Sacred is restored in beauty

Sacred is restored in beauty

Sacred is restored in beauty

Sacred is restored in beauty

REFERENCES

Bachman, R. (1992). *Death and violence on the reservation*. New York: Auburn House.

Beck, P. V., & Walters, A. L. (1977). *The sacred, ways of knowledge sources of life.* Tsailee, AZ: Navajo Community College Press.

Braveheart-Jordan, M., & DeBruyn, L.(1995). *So she may walk in balance: Integrating the impact of historical trauma in the treatment of Native American Indian Women.* In J. Adleman & G. Enguidanos (Eds), *Racism in the lives of women* (pp. 123-153). New York: Hawthorne Press.

Duran, E. F. & Duran, B. M. (1995). *Native American post colonial psychology.* New York: SUNY Press.

Matthews, W. (1994). *Navajo legends.* Salt Lake City: University of Utah Press.

Morgan, R. (1983). *The Iatrogenics handbook.* Toronto: IPI Press.

Opler, M. E. (1938). *Myths and tales of the Jicarilla Apache Indians.* Lincoln, NE: University of Nebraska Press.

Spivak, G. (1988). Can the subaltern speak. In C. Grossberg & N. L. Grossberg (Eds.), *Marxism and the interpretation of culture.* Urbana: University of Illinois Press.

Zolbrod, P. G. (1984). *Dine bahane, The Navajo creation story.* Albuquerque, NM: University of New Mexico Press.

6

Asian-American Domestic Violence: A Critical Psychohistorical Perspective

Benjamin R. Tong*

THE LEGEND OF THE WOMAN WARRIOR, FAH MUK LANN (RETOLD BY BENJAMIN R. TONG)

Centuries ago, in Imperial China, a famous charismatic warrior living in retirement, General Hua, received orders from the emperor to report for active duty immediately. He was to join a huge battle already in progress, intended to repel a powerful invading enemy force on the northernmost borders of the country.

His family was alarmed. The general was coming along in years and not in the best of health. What was he to do?

It was certain that Hua's only son, Mu Li, could not take his place, for the boy was much too young for combat. His daughter, Fah Muk Laan, a young girl in her twenties, had mastered the arts of fighting and strategy from her father, but women in those days were not permitted to serve in the armed forces.

For an entire sleepless night, Muk Laan struggled within her mind and heart for an answer. Near dawn, when the time was at hand for General Hua to depart for the front lines, she appeared before the family in full battle regalia. Muk Laan announced that she, in fact, would take her father's place. She insisted that she could pass for her brother and could, therefore, represent the family in the war effort.

Upset and concerned, her parents immediately objected to the well-intended, but obviously dangerous, idea. In the end, however, General

*© 1993 Institute for the Study of Social Change, University of California, Berkeley

and Mrs. Hua's attempts to dissuade their fiercely determined daughter proved to be ineffective. With tears in their eyes, they reluctantly gave their consent and blessings, urging her to take every precaution. Bidding farewell, Fah Muk Laan mounted a battle steed and rode off toward the northern border.

Upon arrival at the front lines, Muk Laan succeeded in passing as her brother. In the weeks and months to follow, she impressed her fellow soldiers with the superb abilities she had acquired from years of training with her father. Soon her feats of courage and strategy resulted in rapid promotions, until finally she became commanding general.

The fighting went on for nearly a decade until, in one critical campaign, Fah Muk Laan decisively defeated the enemy, driving all survivors back across the border, for a long time, if not, indeed, for good. When she led her victorious troops back to the capital city, the emperor offered Muk Laan an even higher position in the government. With polite diplomacy, she declined, requesting simply that she be allowed to return home. It had been, after all, 10 years since she had last seen her family and village.

The time was finally at hand to reveal to her companions in combat that she was really a woman. When she changed from military garb to a woman's outfit, all who thought they knew her well were deeply surprised. From that day forward the Legend of Fah Muk Laan was born and spread throughout the land for generations thereafter.

There is hardly anything resembling an extensive and informative work on who abuses whom in Asian American households, and how often and, most important of all, why. If such a body of work actually exists, I myself have not seen it, save for a scant few articles. Yet if people on the clinical frontlines know what they have witnessed, domestic violence does indeed go on. Only in recent years have we seen a few suggestive articles and essays, written in a general vein, hinting at a factual basis for the phenomenon, but with scarcely any kind of demographic or empirical documentation (e.g., Chan, 1988; Christensen, 1988; Hirata, 1979; Ho, 1990; Ocampo, 1989; Root, 1985; Tsui, 1985). There is a glaring paucity of hard data with respect to prevalence and incidence.

Because the present chapter is necessarily of limited scope (as opposed to a much more comprehensive, multivolume book-length discussion), I will select one Asian American group—Chinese Americans—as a focus for

---

[1]Chinese, Japanese, Korean, Pilipino, Burmese, Vietnamese, Laotian, Kampuchian (Cambodian), Mien, Miao, Asian Indian, Malaysian, Thai, Indonesian, Hawaiian, Fijian, Samoan, Guamanian, Okinawan.

observations on the psychohistorical roots of domestic violence. The reader is invited to consider the proposition that in certain respects related experiences of other Asian Americans might well be compellingly similar if not entirely identical.

There are, at last count, 19 culturally distinct Asian American communities.[1] It would certainly not do for me to couch my comments in general "Asian American" terms and, in the process, imply that experiences presumably common to all 19 are somehow more significant than the differences between those groups. Such is not the case. The very same observers who would insist on the obvious convenience of such overgeneralizations would, in another instance, be appalled at the notion that all European cultures are necessarily identical or more similar than different; that is, growing up in Luxemborg is no different than a childhood in London.

Restricting my attention to Chinese Americans, I invite the reader to decide, if he or she is able to, the extent to which my remarks might have wider relevance vis-à-vis other Americans of Asian descent. For the balance of this discussion, I will argue that the etiological roots of domestic abuse—whether physical, emotional, or sexual—are to be found in four interrelated phenomena: problems of adaptation, cross-cultural clashes, racist oppression, and repressive heritage.

ADAPTATIONAL PROBLEMS

Massive Asian immigration since the mid-1960s has received a great deal of attention as of late, prompting many to conclude that Asian America consists, by and large, of so-called recent newcomers.[2] Hence, the understandable media, scholarly, and social service priority given to adaptational problems of immigrants. According to federal Census Bureau surveys for the years 1975 to 1985, almost half of the 4.7 million Asian, Hispanic, and Black people who moved to the United States from abroad in that period settled in suburban and nonmetropolitan areas, obviously making for adaptational struggles of an unprecedented nature (Herbers, 1986). When Chinese as well as other Asian newcomers encounter the demands of everyday life in the United States, values, beliefs, and norms are "compared," or "shaken," or "broken up," or "tried on for size," or "imposed," depending on one's way of understanding such experiences.

---

[2]Of the 570,000 immigrants who entered this country legally in the year 1985, 46% were Asian, while 37% were Latin American, 11% European, 3% African, and 2% Canadian (Herbers, 1986).

Regardless of interpretation, discerning observers have noted that domestic stress, which often enough leads to conflict and abuse, is frequently traceable to such newcomer issues as language difficulties, status anxieties, money hassles, pressures to perform well at school and work, abrupt and unprecedented shifts in traditional family roles, and separation or loss of significant others (Huang & Ying, 1989; Lee, 1982; Shon & Ja, 1982; Wong, 1988).

> The Lee family came from Hong Kong about 4 years ago. Neither parent has had the opportunity to learn English, as between father and mother there are a total of four part-time blue-collar jobs. The children are now of middle and high school age. They, too, work, when not keeping school hours, to help supplement the family income. Whenever strangers appear at the front door (e.g., police, mail deliverers, solicitors, survey researchers), the children assume responsibility for being interpreters and translators. Sometimes they even make major decisions for the entire family as a result of this special role of spokespersons with representatives of the outside world. Lately, Mr. Lee has been unusually cranky, irritable, and emotionally abusive of both spouse and children. A neighbor recently reported seeing Mr. Lee slap his oldest child during a heated argument in front of their house, "something which seemed unusual for him to do."

In his deliberations on the nature of myth and identity, Bruner (1979) offered a psychohistorical paradigm that might well serve to account for a significant volume of symptomatic behavior—including domestic violence—related to the stresses of the migration experience. A people's deepest beliefs and worldviews, or mythos, provide for a coherent narrative to address three fundamental concerns that cut across collective existence as well as individual lives: (1) history, a sense of the past, or "who we have always been"; (2) identity, a sense of the present, or "who are, or should be, right now"; and (3) destiny, a sense of the future, or "who we are meant to be." Events like war, economic chaos, and natural disasters disrupt the substance and continuity of all three. Furthermore, migration aimed at escaping the consequences of such catastrophic events exacerbate that very same disruption. Sluski's (1979) rather eloquent "stage" theory of migratory adjustments suggests something of the impact on family structure and dynamics.

> Some families manage to mourn what has been left behind and integrate it constructively into a blend of old and new rules, models, and habits that constitute their new reality. . . . In other families, whatever has been left behind in the country of origin, may become increasingly idealized (making adaptation more difficult) or denigrated (making mourning and working through of the loss more difficult). (p. 386)

THE CLASH OF CULTURES
AND CULTURAL DOMINATION

Scholars and clinicians alike have observed, if we may stay with Sluski's (1979) perspective, that modern Western psychotherapists tend to be positively oriented toward such White middle-class values as differentiation and independence of family members, but "in families of other cultures, however—Southern Italians, Arabs, Chinese, among others—mutual dependence may be equated with loyalty, and any attempt at increasing the independence of members will be considered an attack on basic family values" (p. 388).

In many, if not most, Asian American homes, whether newly arrived or otherwise, children, particularly females, are expected to perform all manner of chores and tasks with precision and thoroughness. Whereas failure to comply in a White middle-class family might mean loss of television-viewing privileges for a time, Asian American children "falling down on the job" are frequently told, as Wong-Fillmore and Cheong's research (1976) on the early socialization of Asian American female offspring has documented, that they are basically worthless as human beings.

> To do well on a task, on the other hand, does not bring praise or reward. Instead, the parent is likely to say nothing at all. Praise is considered emotional excess and in bad taste, and to be avoided, especially where girls are concerned. Thus, the female (child) can hope only for silence, which might be taken as a sign of non-disapproval—or the next best thing to approval. (p. 8)

From the vantage point of contemporary mental health standards, this kind of parenting smacks of that brand of domestic violence known as emotional abuse. I for one could not agree more, which, I would argue, does not necessarily make me culturally insensitive or biased. In the view of this Asian American health practitioner, the devastating psychological consequences of certain child-rearing customs, however longstanding, mitigate against according respect and honor to such practices.

If viewed in terms of a continuum of disciplinary behaviors, procedures like severe physical beatings resulting in broken limbs and profuse bleeding are almost universally defined across "normal" American ethnic and cultural groups as truly abusive. A few notches up from that polar extreme, however, we encounter a definitional gray zone. Sending a child to bed without supper may seem, to White middle-class parents, quite appropriate for misbehavior, while Asian Americans might very well judge that very same procedure ("starving a child") to be inhumanly deprivational. Similarly, many Asian Americans regard whacking a child on the buttocks or behind the thighs as appropriate, all the while educated White middle-class parents remain vehement about any and all forms of corporal punishment as physically abusive.

My own stance here is that given such quandaries, parents and health professionals alike cannot avoid certain inescapable existential decisions as to what is right and wrong. To be sure, it is not a simple matter of taking cultural "sides." In my mind, whatever leads to psychological injury or impairment *is* abuse, no matter how "traditional" the practice. Despite the risk of cultural imperialism, culture is not to be exalted in every instance as sacred and beyond question. It should be borne in mind that, more often than not, people emigrate from other shores in order to escape cultural traditions experienced as oppressive. I shall have more to say about this complex and delicate issue in the section on "Repressive Heritage."

The clash of cultures also results in identity problems, both fake and real. This is a phenomenon that, I would argue, results in many instances of domestic violence. According to Frank Chin and Jeffrey Paul Chan (1972), in their famous essay, "Racist Love," White America dominates Yellow America by defining the content and parameters of our existence. Asian Americans learn, early on, that we are supposedly caught in the vice of a unique identity problem, namely, the problem of having only two options for answering the question "Who am I?"

Asian Americans must necessarily see themselves as either "Asians," meaning perpetual aliens on these shores, or "Americans," meaning "imitation whites." According to this either-or or "dual personality" mindset, we are to assume that (1) Asian Americans, being foreigners, do not belong in the United States, and (2) the word *American* applies exclusively to whites, the alleged "real" Americans. Moreover, Asian America as a unique, vital, self-generating way of life unto itself must be assumed to not exist. We are seen as having no history, literature, language, mythology, or sensibility all our own.

Asian Americans are frequently singled out as the "model minority," the ideal racial pets of White America. So long as our behavior is aligned with the "racist love" stereotype of passive, industrious, noncomplaining, meek and mild servants, the White power structure rewards us. Assertive, aggressive, outspoken, confident, sensuous behavior invites White "racist hate," the kind meted out to people of color in America who dare challenge White authority. Whether forever foreigner or fake white, Asian Americans are expected to be hardworking, inexpressive, compliant, and generally invisible, all the while euphemizing constricted personality as the legacy of an exotic, effeminate, little-understood ancestral "Oriental" culture (see also Tong, 1971, 1974, 1978, 1983b, 1990). The end result is a well-behaved, self-monitoring "model minority" caught in the jaws of such cruel disparities as that between high educational achievements (as measured by acquisition of degrees and credentials), on the one hand, and low income level and workplace status (when compared with Whites), on the other (Cabezas, 1990; Hong, 1988).

> Mr. Wong, 39, a senior accounting clerk of many years at City Hall, was reportedly distraught over a blocked promotion, an experience apparently not new to him or Asian American coworkers in his department and throughout the civil service system. For an entire week, he drank rather heavily at the end of the work day. One evening, his wife was treated at County Hospital's emergency services for facial bruises, the result of what was initially described as an unfortunate "home accident" ("I tripped and fell on a couple of boxes that were near the bottom of the basement stairs," Mrs. Wang explained.) Later, Mrs. Wong confided to a sympathetic female paramedic that her husband had actually struck her when he "lost control of himself" in the course of venting rage about yet another frustrated attempt at a deserved promotion.

> When he finally agreed to try couples counseling with a culturally competent therapist, Mr. Wong said, "I do as I'm told, y'know, I do good work. I'm always reliable. And I'm not like other people who make a lot of noise, do a lot of fancydan office politics to get what they want. I've just done my job, as best as I know how. Never complained, not even when I felt like it. And, boy, there were plenty of times when I felt like it! I'd always hoped, always expected, my supervisor would notice that I deserved a promotion to middle manager. I mean, I am fully qualified. Some of my coworkers would even say more than fully qualified. So what do I get? Nothing! The word is that they say my accent is too heavy, and that I just don't look or act or sound like a management type. They say that a manager or executive type has to be an 'American.' So what does that make me? Hell, I've never left this country! Am I some alien from outer space with an incurably thick foreign accent? After all these years, I'm insulted by being asked to *train* a new guy, a white man, who's supposed to get the management position I deserved. What the hell, I mean, that was really the last straw. I can't take it anymore."

RACIST OPPRESSION

When dealing with the question of domestic violence, we must address, as standard clinical practice usually dictates, the need to "take a history." If we were to take a history of perpetrators of Asian American domestic violence, we would find an abundance of evidence for "early experiences" of abuse. Victimizers, more often than not, were victims at one time. This, as we know only too well, is a well-established truism in clinical work. The compelling "psychohistorical" studies of eminent scholars like Robert Jay Lifton have made it abundantly clear that human beings overwhelmed by successive, multiple experiences of uncontrollable brutality will themselves become, in short order, monstrous perpetrators of heinous violence, as we have come to learn in such wartime atrocities as the infamous My Lai Massacre (Lifton, 1983, esp. chap. 12).

Long before an Asian American abuses spouse or children, he had already suffered flagrant and wholesale abuse. This preceding history is not simply traceable to troubles in that universe of experience known as "family of origin": it is at the same time bound up with nothing less than the entire fabric of Asian American history and culture itself. Put another way, the full range of violence experienced by Asian Americans must first be acknowledged and situated in proper context.

For example, I have long held the position that the life of virtually every Asian American group has been marked by at least one major episode of what might be called "collective racist trauma," an experience of White violence so thoroughly inundating that it functions up to the present day as a central point of reference for making sense of themselves in America (Tong, 1971, 1974, 1978, 1983b). It is the ground from which arises the raw material for language, myth, and metaphor that an entire people struggles to forge in order to codify and deal with that trauma.

For Pilipino America, it was the brutal colonial subjugation of the Philippine Islands at the turn of the century; for Japanese America, the concentration camps of World War II. For Korean wives of White American servicemen, it was the alienation and abuse of dysfunctional post–Korean War interracial marriages. For Vietnamese America, it was the intervention of the United States in a civil war between the Vietnamese. And for Chinese America, it was the infamous Anti-Chinese Movement (1785–1943) (Kim, 1980; Kuwabara, 1992; Lawson, 1989; Lott, 1974; Nagata, 1988; Nakamura, 1970; Nee & Nee, 1970; Owan, Bliatout, Lin, Nguyen, & Wong, 1985; Takaki, 1989; tenBroek et al., 1954; Tong, 1983a; Weglyn, 1976).

In recent years, it might be noted, anti-Asian American sentiment and violence have been on the rise throughout the United States (Chin, 1992; Hing, 1990). Presently, hate-motivated crimes against Asian Americans break down into four recurrent types, according to John Hayakawa Torok of the New York City–based Committee Against Anti-Asian Violence (Cacas, 1992, p. 26):

- Police misconduct: police use racial slurs or other offensive language.
- Neighborhood-based aggression: Asians moving into a neighborhood are made to feel uncomfortable as a result of acts such as throwing garbage on the front lawn or offensive language.

- Random attacks by civilians on buses or in the street: verbal assaults through the use of racial slurs or threatened physical harm and actual attacks.
- Abusive behavior in schools: classmates react to teachers' labeling Asians as "model" students by verbally harassing, physically attacking, or robbing Asian students.

REPRESSIVE HERITAGE

If one would take a truly comprehensive "clinical history" of domestic violence in the Chinese American as well as other Asian American communities, it would be necessary to attend not only to Asian American but also Asian "roots" with a critical eye. The long record of the Chinese experience is replete with countless instances of the violence of a cruel patriarchal social order (Fairbank, 1974), ostensibly attributable to Confucius, the greatest and most revered of China's ancient sages. Power, influence, and authority resided exclusively in adult males, beginning with fathers and teachers and, finally, government officials and the emperor. "Negative" emotions were to be impounded in public, particularly in the presence of male authority figures. Respect for authority was equated with unconditional obedience. Moreover, the family came first, and everything and everyone else was insignificant or not even real. Women were allowed a modicum of power, provided they lived long enough to become mothers-in-law and grandmothers. Then the abused became abusers (Stacey, 1983).

By the time of the last dynasty, the Ch'ing (A.D. 1644–1911), monarchic and scholar-official politics had reshaped the classical Confucian concept of *pao-tia*, "taking care of one's own," into an insidious device for social control. It was an officially imposed but unofficial arm of the state, through which the government and local ruling class used the family system for political purposes (Fairbank & Reischauer, 1960). Under the *pao-tia* system, redefined as "local order through mutual responsibility," the family was the basic unit of political control and kept the individual in line with such psychological devices as fear of punishment and moral exhortation.

A group of households was accountable all together for an individual within any household. "This allotment of responsibility by groups of neighboring farms was particularly suited to a static society rooted in the land. . . . Mutual responsibility, as totalitarian systems have . . . demonstrated, is a powerful device, especially when combined with a paternalistic morality sanctioned by a long cultural tradition" (Fairbank & Reischauer, 1960, pp. 374–375). In other words, the ruling elites controlled the peasantry and commoner populace by having people in villages continually turn on one another. Resentment or rage toward the government was "safely" deflected or projected onto less powerful family members and neighbors.

The constant distrust, intimidation, jealousies, isolation, and control maneuvers made for what psychotherapists today would call a kind of classic "abuse dynamic." It is against this psychohistorical backdrop that Chinese and even Chinese American domestic violence is to be understood. Many a Chinese American has suffered massive emotional ambivalence about whether such a repressive, and most certainly violent, "heritage" deserves to be preserved.

It bears noting that Chinese Americans (and countless Chinese as well) have been operating on the highly questionable assumption that this "traditional" autocratic, quasi-military family system, dating back some two thousand years to the early dynasties of the Han emperors, is somehow continuous with the original ("classic") humanistic teachings and vision of Confucius. The historical record indicates, however, that nothing could be further from the truth.

The Confucius of antiquity is not the Sage of the scholar-official ruling elite, who centuries following his death reworked his ideas for purposes of social control. Sinologists are in general agreement that the ruling groups of imperial China exploited Confucian philosophy as a potent device for controlling a numerically overwhelming commoner population. Balaz (1964), for one, observed that

> [t]he scholar-officials and their state found in Confucianist doctrine an ideology that suited them perfectly . . . in Han times, shortly after the formation of the empire, it became a state doctrine. The virtues preached by Confucianism were exactly suited to the new hierarchical state: respect, humility, docility, obedience, submission, and subordination to elders and betters. (p. 18)

In Arthur Wright's (1960) authoritative work, we learn of convincing documentation, much like that produced by Balaz (1964) and others, that

> [a]s a consequence of major social and political changes beginning in the late T'ang and continuing through the Sung, the content of one of the Confucian moral norms, "loyalty," was radically altered. From its earlier meaning as an obligation tempered by moral judgment, it was redefined as a blind and unquestioning allegiance to a superior. This shift and others related to it occurred under the pressure of an increasingly centralized and despotic monarchy. (p. 5)

This refashioned Confucianism eventually became the official religion of the Chinese state and the ideological framework within which the government operated. This was the moral order imposed on the Southern Chinese during the T'ang era, when the previously unconquered Yueh people, aboriginal ancestors of the Cantonese and today's Cantonese Americans,[3] were subdued. Miyakawa probably has the last word on the phenomenon in his essay "The Confucianization of South China" (In Wright, 1960): "It cannot be said, however, that Confucianism Confucianized the southern peoples solely by functioning as a religion. Its religious function was supported by military and political power of Chinese dynasties, and by local officials and literati (p. 41)."

In contrast to the familiar autocratic patriarch of the typical Chinese and Cantonese family, the Ideal Adult as envisioned by Confucius had only the "ambition" of becoming a "true" or "authentic" person (*jun yun*) (Waley, 1958). The eminent Confucian scholar Tu Wei-Ming (1976) wrote that such an individual, "wishing to establish his own character, also establishes the character of others":

> His learning is "for the sake of himself . . . and he does not regard himself an "instrument" . . . , for his mode of existence is to be an end rather than a tool for any external purpose. . . . In fact, no matter how hard he works and how much distance he covers, a true man is, as it were, all the time on the Way (toward enlightened personal development). (p. 115; see also Cleary, 1992)

In closing, we can say that the dark side of the Chinese American experience—and, by implication, the larger Asian American experience—contains unresolved trauma and internalized violence in response to the legacy of the autocratic nightmare of imperial Confucianism, on the one hand, and White racist oppression, on the other. Coupled with the adaptational demands of migration (particularly for recent newcomers) and the conflicts resulting from the clash of cultures and White cultural domination, these powerful forces have shaped the special arena within which Asian American domestic violence, in all its forms, is played out.

REFERENCES

Balaz, E. (1964). *Chinese civilization and bureaucracy: Variations on a theme* (H. M. Wright, Trans.). New Haven, CT: Yale University Press.

---

[3]The earliest Chinese to appear in significant numbers in this country were those of Cantonese (Southern Chinese) descent, a seafaring, highly adventurous people known to continually come and go from the Chinese Empire, establishing "Chinatowns" wherever they settled outside of China, despite imperial edicts (which were seldom enforced) that warned of dire legal consequences. The majority of Chinese Americans today are still those of Cantonese background.

Bruner, J. (1979). *On knowing: Essays for the left hand* (2nd ed). Cambridge: Harvard University Press.

Cabezas, A. (1990). The Asian American today as an economic success model: Some myths and realities. In Chinese for Affirmative Action (Ed.), *Breaking the silence*. San Francisco.

Cacas, S. R. (1992, April 3). Recognizing and responding to hate, violence and bigotry: A survival guide for Asian Pacific Americans. *Asian Week*.

Chan, C. S. (1988). Asian American women: Psychological responses to sexual exploitation and cultural stereotypes. In L. Fulani (Ed.), *The psychopathology of everyday racism and sexism*. New York: Harrington Press.

Chin, F., & Chan, J. P. (1972). Racist love. In R. Kostelanetz (Ed.), *Seeing through Shuck*. New York: Ballantine.

Chin, S. A. (1992, February 28). U.S. study finds wide anti-Asian prejudice. *San Francisco Examiner*.

Christensen, C. P. (1988). Issues in sex therapy with ethnic and racial minority women. *Women and Therapy, 7*(2/3), 187–205.

Cleary, T. (1992). *The essential Confucius: The heart of Confucius' teachings in authentic I-Ching order*. San Francisco: HarperCollins.

Fairbank, J. K. (1974). The United States and China (3rd ed). Cambridge: Harvard University Press.

Fairbank, J. K., & Reischauer, E. (1960). *East Asia: The great tradition*. Boston: Houghton Mifflin.

Herbers, J. (1986, December 14). Many immigrants now bypass cities for suburbs. *New York Times*.

Hing, B. O. (1990). Current factors in the re-emergence of anti-Asian violence. In Chinese for Affirmative Action (Ed.), *Break the silence*. San Francisco.

Hirata, L. C. (1979). Free, indentured, enslaved: Chinese prostitutes in nineteenth-century America. *Signs, Journal of women in Culture and Society, 5*(1), 3–29.

Ho, C. K. (1990). An analysis of domestic violence in Asian American communities: A multicultural approach to counseling. *Women and Therapy, 9*(1/2), 129–150.

Hong, F. (1988, May). Barriers at the top: What invisible barriers keep Asian American executives from climbing the corporate ladder to the top? *ASIAM*.

Huang, L. N., & Ying, Y. W. (1989). Chinese American children and adolescents. In J. T. Gibbs, L. N. Huang, and associates (Eds.), *Children of color: Psychological interventions with minority youth*. San Francisco: Jossey-Bass.

Kim, B. K. L. (1980). Asian wives of U.S. servicemen: Women in shadows. In R. Endo et al. (Eds.), *Asian Americans: Social and Psychological Perspectives* (Vol. 2). Palo Alto, CA: Science and Behavior Books.

Kuwabara, L. (1992, April 15). No denying: R. A. Shiomi's "Uncle Tadao" struggles to sort through the emotional and psychological aftershocks of internment. *San Francisco Bay Guardian*.

Lawson, J. E. (1989). "She's a pretty woman . . . for a gook": The misogyny of the Vietnam War. *Journal of American Culture, 12*(3), 55–63.

Lee, E. (1982). A social systems approach to assessment and treatment for Chinese American families. In M. McGoldrick, J. K. Pearce, & J. Giordano (Eds.), *Ethnicity and family therapy*. New York: Guilford Press.

Lifton, R. J. (1983). *The broken connection: On death and the continuity of life*. New York: Basic Books.

Lott, J. T. (1974). Migration of a mentality: The Pilipino community. *Migration, 2*(6).

Miyakawa, H. (1960). The Confucianization of South China. In A. F. Wright (Ed.), *The Confucian Persuasion*. Palo Alto, CA: Stanford University Press.

Nagata, D. K. (1988, August). The long-term effects of victimization: Present-day effects of the Japanese American internment. In D. Nagata (Chair), *Varied forms of victimization during World War II*. Symposium conducted at the meeting of the American Psychological Association, Atlanta.

Nakamura, N. (1970). The nature of G.I. racism. *Gidra*.

Nee, V., & Nee, B. D. (1973). *Longtime Californ': A documentary study of an American Chinatown*. New York: Pantheon.

Ocampo, B. (1989, August 25). Some battered wives suffer "cycle of abuse." *Asian Week*.

Owan, T. C., Bliatout, B., Lin, K. M., Nguyen, T., & Wong, H. Z. (Eds.). (1985). *Southeast Asian mental health: Treatment, prevention, services, training, and research* (DHHS Publication No. ADM 85-1399). Rockville, MD: National Institute of Mental Health.

Root, M. P. P. (1985). Guidelines for facilitating therapy with Asian American clients. *Psychotherapy, 22* (2 S), 349–356.

Shon, S. P., & Ja, D. Y. (1982). Asian (American) families. In M. McGoldrick, J. K. Pearce, & J. Giordano (Eds.), *Ethnicity and family therapy*. New York: Guilford Press.

Sluski, C. E. (1979). Migration and family conflict. *Family process, 18*(4), 379–390.

Stacey, J. (1983). *Patriarchy and social revolution in China*. Berkeley: University of California Press.

Takaki, R. (1989). *Strangers from a different shore: A history of Asian Americans*. Boston: Little, Brown.

tenBroek, J., et al. (1954). *Prejudice, war and the constitution*. Berkeley and Los Angeles: University of California.

Tong, B. R. (1971). The ghetto of the mind: Notes on the historical psychology of Chinese America. *Amerasia Journal, 1*(2), 1–31.

Tong, B. R. (1974). A living death defended as the legacy of a superior culture. *Amerasia Journal, 2*(2), 178–202.

Tong, B. R. (1978). Warriors and victims: Chinese American sensibility and learning styles. In L. Morris et al. (Eds.), *Extracting learning styles from social/cultural diversity: Studies of five American minorities*. Norman: Southwest Teacher Corps Network, University of Oklahoma.

Tong, B. R. (1983a). Long-term consequences of the Nikkei internment. *East Wind* (Fall/Winter), 51–53.

Tong, B. R. (1983b). On the confusion of psychopathology with culture: Iatrogenesis in the treatment of Chinese Americans. In R. F. Morgan (Ed.), *The Iatrogenics handbook: A critical look at research and practice in the helping professions*. Toronto: IPI Publishing.

Tong, B. R. (1990). "Ornamental Orientals" and others: Ethnic labels in review. *Focus, 4*(2), 8–9.

Tsui, A. M. (1985). Psychotherapeutic considerations in sexual counseling for Asian immigrants. *Psychotherapy, 22*(2 S), 357–362.

Tu Wei-Ming. (1976). The Confucian perception of adulthood. *Daedalus, 105*(2), 109–123.

Waley, A. (1958). *The analects of Confucius*. New York: Grove Press.

Weglyn, M. (1976). *Years of infamy*. New York: William Morrow.

Wong, M. G. (1988). The Chinese American family. In C. H. Mindel, R. W. Haberstein, & R. Wright Jr. (Eds.), *Ethnic families in America: Patterns and variations* (3rd ed.). New York: Elsevier.

Wong-Fillmore, L., & Cheong, J. L. (1976). *The early socialization of Asian American female children*. Paper presented at the Conference on Educational and Occupational Needs of Asian-Pacific American Women, San Francisco.

Wright, A. F. (Ed.). (1960). *The Confucian persuasion*. Palo Alto, CA: Stanford University Press.

7

Asian Men and Violence

Lee Mun Wah

I think that the hardest part of writing about one's life experiences is trying to convey the *feeling* of what happened—at best, we can only describe it, reflect on it, circle the place where our pain began. What I remember of what has taken me to this place where I am right now is only easier to talk about because something greater has come out of it. But the memory of that day never leaves me, and writing about it only refreshes the terror and the difficulty in finding the words for my grief and the depth of my aloneness when it happened. For anyone who has ever been harmed, physically or emotionally, there is no cure, no complete recovery. We remain survivors who are emotionally disabled and like the terminally ill, appreciate more tenderly how close death is to life. What we share is not so much what happened to us, but how it changed our lives and how we struggle daily to cope with the many constant reminders of that moment. An old Buddhist story relates that we all experience pain. Some of us remain bitter and continue to be suspicious of all life, while others decide to be prepared and to accept that pain is also part of life along with joy and birth. I think that both experiences are a part of our journey through any crisis—bitterness that it happened to us, and eventually acceptance. The remembrance of our anguish and our hurt can help us remain vulnerable and hopefully more compassionate toward others. Since my own experience with death, every time I hear about someone dying or murdered, I hold my breath for a moment in honor of their death and of my own someday.

In a way, when I look back to that moment in 1985, there were two deaths, my mother's and my own. She lost her life and I lost a way of living that would never be mine again. I wrote about that year in my diary:

"In the winter of '85, my mother was murdered. She was shot four times in the head. It was a warm Tuesday afternoon." Those are the facts of how she died. In the beginning, whenever I was asked what happened, those were the kinds of answers I would give. It was easier and simpler that way, for me and the person asking. I don't remember a whole lot from that first year, only that I kept crying all the time, on warm days and when something good happened to me. There are so many 'ifs' that I've given up trying to visualize what might have been. What happened changed my whole life and everyone in our family. Even our friends were moved and frightened by the way our mom died. They seemed, like ourselves, to sense the frailty of the moment and strong bond of a mother to her children.

It is so hard for me to let go of her and not to have had the chance to say goodbye and to let her know how much I loved her.

I can only hope she can hear me now. I whisper it every day.

I thought of you, today
falling behind into time
Trying to find your way out of the ground
a seed afire beneath the earth.

And what I realized
is that there is no bed
that can hold back the pain of moving on.

When night falls, it matters not
who leaves
or who chooses to stay.

A great silence comes
to sleep in every room.

What happened during the first year of my mom's death seemed a lot like being frozen and slowly thawing out, as I scratched and crawled my way through the terror of living again inch by inch. Toward the end of the year, on the suggestion of a friend, I joined a men's group. I remember how scared I was being in a room filled with men and just being left to talk about my feelings. Deep down I knew I was in this group because my mother's death brought up how much I was afraid of other men emotionally, spiritually, and physically. I also realized that I had a great deal of anger inside of me toward the man who killed my mom, at myself for not being there to protect her when she died, and at my mother for dying so soon before she had a chance to hold my son in her arms.

In the years that passed I learned a lot about how to trust and to let other men into my life without being afraid or defensive. One day, I got really mad at one of the men in the group. One of the other men said that he thought I wasn't being angry enough. I was furious; I told him that for an Asian man I was really angry. At that moment, I realized that he wanted me to get angry the way a White man got angry. I had never seen an Asian man get angry in public, on television, or in the movies. All my life, the only models I had for getting angry were White men. But somewhere deep inside of me I always knew I could never live up to John Wayne's fury or rage. Too much of my culture held me back as my anger and my rage circled inside of me, longing to scream and to be heard.

Months later, I started an Asian Men's Group to help other Asian American men like myself find a place where they could explore and be supported in expressing their anger and their passion without feeling inadequate or inferior to other cultures. What I learned was that working through anger is not something that can be taught in isolation or without the recognition of one's cultural background. Dealing with anger is a personal and developmental journey that needs to be nurtured and acknowledged for each personal story and struggle. A. S. Neil once observed that children at his Summerhill school cut his classes in proportion to the amount of time they were angry in their previous schools. The children returned when their anger was spent and when they felt they could "choose" to return. I think that somewhere from my own experiences I sensed that these Asian American men in the group needed to feel comfortable and accepted for who they were. They needed to choose to work through their anger at their own pace and in their own way without feeling they needed to be like someone else or sound a certain way. They could also say no when they didn't want to go any further without being judged as passive or being seen as mysterious.

In the months that followed, what I discovered were some of the roots of their anger as well as some of the results of not having their anger expressed or understood. None of the men in the group had ever witnessed anger being resolved in their families. Most of them felt that they would not be heard or would lose control or hurt someone if they really let their anger out. All of them learned about anger from their parents, particularly from their fathers. Each of them wanted and needed to be acknowledged and accepted by his parents for who he was and for what he was doing with his life.

I came to realize after a few weeks that men in the group needed something from myself and the rest of the group that they weren't getting from their families or their communities—acknowledgment and support to explore their fears, their anger, their relationships, their hurt, their dreams, and their desires. So what I did was to create a "container" that would enable each man in the group to feel listened to and acknowledged. I did this by creating a number of exercises on how to deal with conflict so that the men in the group would feel safe with each other and also feel that there was a way they could express their anger without hurting anyone physically. We then explored the relationship that the men had with their fathers and how their fathers affected how they related to others today. We also dealt with the issue of racism and the affect it had on the men in the group. Essentially, we covered three important areas: their individual lives, their family histories, and the effects of the community on their development. Finally, I had the men invite their families and friends to an acknowledgment ceremony. This ceremony was to enable the men in the group to hear from their loved ones how much they cared for them and what they best remembered about them.

We have been meeting since 1985, one night a week for three hours. In that time, we have grown and we have changed. We have shared our lives with each other and we have become a family. One man in the group described it perfectly: "This group is like my family. Maybe even better than my family because, here, I can start all over fresh. I can say things here that I wouldn't anywhere else, and still be accepted week after week. No one will leave me because I said something or did something wrong. In some ways, you guys are a lot closer to me than my own family. You are the family I always wanted."

CONFLICT RESOLUTION

"If you don't like what I'm saying, you can step outside later and I'll show you what I'm *not* saying!" When one of the men said this to another man in a violence workshop I was facilitating, I realized that he was angry and hurt because he didn't feel seen or heard (a recurrent theme in his marriage and family of origin). The only means he knew of for expressing his anger was to use violence. So often anger is not the primary emotion; rather it is the feeling of being hurt that comes first, hurt at not being listened to or acknowledged. And so the anger is about not having one's hurt be seen or validated. Men who are violent are often unable or don't know how to clearly state that they are hurt, and so they resort to violence.

Before any of the men begin to work on a conflict, I ask them whether or not they want to resolve this conflict or simply to win. I do this so that their intentions are clear and so is the desired outcome. So often we enter into a battle without any vision, except that we're angry, not knowing where we want to go or where we want to end up. In the battle of trying to win, there is always a loser, and if that is their intention, it is important to be sure that each person involved is willing to be the loser or the winner.

In the Japanese culture, when one enters into a conflict, the relationship is held to be what is most important, to be preserved, not the individual. The role of the Japanese community is to help those involved to keep this as their focus and goal. When the community order is honored, the culture remains intact and protected. The American approach often emphasizes the individual interest as the most important goal, even if it means sacrificing the relationship. In many ways there is a lot to be said for the Japanese perspective of not humiliating someone to the point that they feel isolated or in danger of having their integrity questioned in public. The term "losing face" is about humiliation and disgrace.

Once in the group, one of the men yelled back at me when I asked him what he was willing to give up to resolve a conflict. He said, "I'm tired of always having to give up something! People of color always have to give up something, and I'm tired of it!" And so I asked him what it was he wanted to keep. And he replied, "I want to keep my integrity. I want the other person to honor my integrity." The essential message here is that when someone feels he is going to lose something or have something he holds dear be destroyed or diminished, he will become defensive and attack.

Before anyone can share how "hurt" he feels, he often needs to release the anguish first. To do so, the environment needs to feel safe. In our group, I work with both men on first deciding if the space between them is comfortable and safe. To Asians and to many other men of color, feeling physically too far away or too close has a lot to do with trust and whether or not they feel threatened. In addition, Asians, like other men of color, often aren't asked what they *need* to feel comfortable. They are usually *told* how to accommodate or they are simply left to react, and that is usually defensively. So, given an opportunity to decide what is the best distance is a beginning in the conflict where each man feels listened to and in control of his life.

After the men have shared what is a comfortable distance (and that may require some negotiating), they are asked to have a moment of silence to "observe" how they are feeling and how the other person is feeling. I also ask them to notice where they feel closed or hurt. To Asians, so much is said nonverbally, that a lot can be learned.

In our group, there are four steps that lead to conflict resolution: stating why you are angry, how and why you were hurt, what you need from the other person to heal, and what you are willing to offer to the other person to begin the healing process. To begin the negotiation process, one agrees to begin while the other person listens without interruption. When the man speaking is finished, the listener must repeat back what he as heard and ask if there is anything he has left out. If he has, the speaker will let him know what is missing, and the listener repeats it back until everything is accurately stated.

This process is essential to any kind of conflict resolution—accurately acknowledging what is said. Acknowledgment is the first step in feeling validated. So often when we hear why someone is mad at us, we selectively shut out what we don't want to hear or we change what we decide to hear. I know that when I get involved in a conflict I sometimes stop hearing what's being said and start preparing how I'm going to defend myself. Repeating back what we have heard gives both persons a chance to know that they are being heard. This doesn't mean that both persons have to agree with what they hear, but that they are open to listening to the other's concerns. The Buddhist would call this honoring another person's heart.

So often I have seen the men's fears calmed when they both agreed that they wanted to resolve their conflict. I remember a professor in college who asked his classes every year whether or not they had ever witnessed a conflict resolved in their families. No one had raised their hands in all those years. It seemed so sad to recognize that we all came from families where conflicts weren't resolved, but it also brought up a sense of compassion and understanding why so many conflicts are left unresolved. We all go as far as the extent of our experiences. As a Chinese philosopher once said, "To go in a new direction, we have to take a different path."

So how does the Asian American man express his anger? How does he reconcile the Asian culture with his American counterpart? These are not easy questions to answer or to recognize. I remember the words of the Asian men when they walked into the room for their first meeting. They all said, "This is like coming home to all your brothers, knowing that you'll be understood and you won't have to explain certain things all the time. Everyone will just understand because they went through the same thing and they know how it feels." But the world outside our group is not the same ethnicity, and so we all have to cope with that difference and our uniqueness.

Being an Asian American is a special culture in itself because it carries the seeds of two worlds. One man in our group described it perfectly. He said, "Here, in America, I'm always faced with never being fully accepted because I'm Japanese and not White. I went back to Japan to reclaim my roots, but once I got there I felt odd and out of place. They saw me as an American. I'm proud of my Japanese heritage, but I didn't fit there either. So who am I?"

There are useful tools and lessons to be learned from both cultures and also tremendous contradictions that have to be dealt with to survive. I remember working for the Shanti Project as a facilitator and being purposely interrupted to see how I would deal with the situation. I remember stopping each time I was interrupted and waiting for the other person to finish talking. No matter how hard I tried I just couldn't interrupt him. There were so many levels of emotions that I felt at that moment. I couldn't interrupt him because, to me, that would be disrespectful. At the same time, I felt that he was being disrespectful to me and that my silence would be seen by him as a sign of how hurt I felt. He didn't notice my silence or he chose to ignore me, which made me feel unseen by a White man once again and also how different I was to other White men. Their persistence of the director to have me "break through something" made me feel like I was not good enough and surely not as bold as White men are. In retrospect, I remember feeling angry at the humiliation and at myself for not meeting their expectations. I felt that I had somehow failed an important ritual of "becoming an American," which most often means not being like a White American man.

My nonacceptance by the White culture also brought up my not feeling accepted by the Chinese community, because I wasn't born in China and I didn't speak my native language. I remembered being called a "banana" (white on the inside and yellow on the outside) and later as "empty bamboo" (Chinese on the outside but empty of tradition and language on the inside). Both terms made me feel isolated and alone.

I remember sharing with an all-White therapists' group that I felt reluctant to talk because even though I would raise my hand to speak next, someone else would interrupt me without being recognized by the facilitator. What was worse was that nobody noticed that I hadn't had a chance to speak. There always seemed to be this sense of urgency in this group that if someone didn't get to speak immediately, he would lose any chance of ever speaking again. I told them of a story I heard about a group of Hawaiian teachers who were asked by their White colleagues why they never spoke and they replied, "Because you never stop talking!"

What I learned from sharing this with my White colleagues was that there was a need to educate and to inform them about Asian ways of listening and sharing that could allow for more dialogue and greater participation from everyone. Most of them agreed and were willing to try things differently. They also really appreciated my saying something. Deep down I would have liked it if they had noticed my pain and spoken up, but perhaps that will happen in the future. For now, it seems that my work is in sharing how I feel unseen and unheard as it happens, just as this chapter and the book as a whole may serve the same purpose. Speaking out may not be safe, but it is necessary.

What I believe that I offer, and the purpose of the Asian Men's Group, is to say that we, as Asians, don't have to imitate the White culture or to be ashamed of our Asian ancestry. There are valuable traits of the Asian culture that are useful and beautiful and that can add and enhance the American culture. What I see is the need for the American culture to respect and not to judge that other cultures that are different are automatically inferior. What is needed is a community of ideas and a welcoming of a diversity of perspectives. Being different can be a thing of beauty and not an obstacle. How we choose to see the world determines how the world perceives us.

Creating as an individual, speaking up for individual rights, and standing up when we experience unjust institutions or corrupt politicians are only a part of the beauty of being born in America. Just as the usefulness in the Asian culture of noticing the words spoken by the face and body, waiting and watching to be sure that everyone had a chance to speak, not interrupting until someone has finished speaking, honoring our communities and our family is important.

FATHER ISSUE

One of the more intense workshops was about our fathers. So much of how the men in the group viewed themselves was defined by how they felt about their fathers. They were looking for a male mentor who would give them all the things that their fathers couldn't. The most common need was for acceptance. More specifically, they wanted assurances from their fathers that they were proud of their sons and felt good about what they were doing with their lives.

Recently, I had the men write down five failures that they had experienced and to come back in a week to share their list with the entire group. I did this exercise on failure because one of the men shared how difficult it was for him to tell the group about why he was fired from a previous job. He was afraid that the group would somehow look down on him or think less of him. I felt that this failure exercise could somehow take away some of the shame as well as foster support and acceptance among the men that failure was an important and natural part of life.

When the whole group did this failure exercise as homework, they discovered that they were more attuned to their failures and less able to get in touch with their successes. Often the men in the group felt that they weren't doing enough and had they been better prepared they wouldn't have failed. The Asian American men talked about feeling family pressures from their fathers and mothers to always act responsibly and to be prepared—to watch out for failure. There was always this sense that relatives and the community were watching and judging their actions. One of the men pointed out that his father never talked about his failures, but he also never talked about his successes.

The men in the group weren't sure why their fathers didn't share their failures or successes with them, but they did feel that when their fathers talked about being oppressed and being put down by society they felt unprotected and open to the same kinds of racism that their fathers had experienced. Somewhere there was this inadvertent message from their fathers to not let their guard down or they would be harmed and humiliated by the White man. When I continually heard this from my father about Whites, I kept wondering to myself, how could I trust that Whites would honor my efforts or accept my shortcomings if they didn't accept my father, whom was more powerful and experienced that I was? I think that at that moment of my recognition about racism towards Asians, I was angry at the world at being so untrustworthy. I was also feeling betrayed by my father who I had always thought was invincible and protective. I was left with this anger and sense of helplessness that I couldn't express or share with my father. I've often wondered if my father felt that way too, as a young man. Maybe the only way he knew how to express his anger as he became a father was to warn me about the dangers of trusting anyone outside the family.

So often the men's movement, as described by Robert Bly and others, ignores that men of color aren't just dealing with relationships with their fathers, but also the impact that White America has had on their fathers that affected how they dealt with their sons. My father taught me that the world was not a safe place to compete with the White man or to show him anger. Standing up to the White man could mean your job, your chances of promotion, and, in many cases, even your life. He told me never to offend White people or to share any family secrets with them because Whites could not be trusted and might someday use that information against me or our family.

My father also told me to use my education and my wealth as a way of telling Whites that I was better than they were. What he was indirectly saying to me was that I should keep my anger and my hurt to myself. My wealth and my position in life and not my words would be my revenge and my sword. What I learned from my father was that my survival was dependent on my silence and my ability to blend in and to support the White society's values and rules. After all, this was America, and being American meant imitating the White man's ways. We were Chinese, the White man was "American."

It isn't surprising, then, that Asian men have a difficult time expressing their successes and their failures. What they need are assurances from others that their disclosures can be expressed safely, with acceptance and with honor. The kind of safely that I am speaking about requires that there be trust and compassion on the part of the listener. The listener needs to be supportive and acknowledging and not to interrupt with his or her stories or judgments.

FATHER WORKSHOP

The Asian men dress up like their fathers and come to the group. We spend a few prior meetings discussing how it feels to ask their fathers for something, as well as how it feels to reveal to their fathers *why* they need their clothing. Very often, exercises like these bring up old issues of how to communicate with their fathers as well as fears of bringing up old feelings that haven't been resolved. What was interesting was that some of the men communicated through their mothers instead of their fathers to get their fathers' clothing. They seemed to feel safer asking their mothers instead of their fathers, for fear their fathers would laugh at them or not understand.

The men whose fathers had passed away were asked to find clothing that most looked like the type their fathers wore. Having the men play their fathers who had passed away was healthy for the group for several reasons. One, it allowed the other men whose fathers were still alive to deal with their fears of their fathers dying before they had a chance to reconcile with them. Two, it gave the men whose fathers had passed away an opportunity to deal with some of their grief and anguish at not having their fathers here when they needed them.

Each man who played his "father" was asked to talk about his son (which was himself) and how he experienced their relationship. The "fathers" were also asked to reveal what it was like for them in their families when they were growing up. In the end, each "father" was asked to share with us some wise words that maybe he had wished his father had said to him. When the "fathers" shared their wise words with their sons, it was the kind of acceptance and acknowledgment the men in the group had always dreamed that their fathers would give them. For others, it gave them an opportunity to reveal what they had always felt too vulnerable to ask from their fathers for fear of rejection or abandonment.

This father exercise is important because it affords an opportunity to return to a place where the men in the group felt stuck or good about their fathers, and from there they would perhaps gain some insight into how their relationship with their fathers affects how they are with others today. It also gave the Asian men in the group a chance to receive acceptance and acknowledgment from their "fathers" so they didn't have to go around looking for a father substitute. Too often, we as men carry a "hidden expectation" that a particular man in our lives will heal our father wounds, only to be disappointed and angry again when that man fails us or doesn't give us exactly what we need.

In learning about their father's past as well as how they perceived their sons, the Asian men gained some compassion for their fathers' struggle through his perception of their relationship. The men in the group were surprised at how much they knew about their fathers' family histories. When the men in the group came to understand that their fathers were only coming from their own experiences, there was an opportunity for acceptance. Sometimes accepting our fathers means accepting them for who they are without any changes. I remember that when I did this father exercise I was surprised to recognize how much I wanted my father to "accept" me without any changes, but I insisted on him changing before I could accept him. It was a humbling acknowledgment about the part I played in our relationship.

ACKNOWLEDGMENT CEREMONY

The acknowledgment ceremony is an opportunity for the group to invite their parents and friends to come and acknowledge them and to share any memorable stories about their relationship together. I found it to be especially important for Asian men and for men of color because it centers on the need for community support and acknowledges the importance of the family.

The ceremony requires a consensus, because each man is needed to participate and to be willing to let it be known in the community that he is a member of this group. Some of the men felt apprehensive about sharing such an intimate experience with their parents. Since 1986, the group has had an acknowledgment ceremony every year. One of the Asian men expressed it quite well. He said, "It's scary to invite your parents here because this has been a special place I come to every Monday night. It's like we're being intruded on and I don't want strangers to come into my home. And yet I know what we've been doing here has been really revolutionary and breaking new ground for Asian men. It's just hard to share that with my friends. I'm afraid they might not understand what I'm doing here, and I'll be embarrassed. What if they don't want to come?"

At first, I had a lot of apprehension about how this ceremony could change the group and all the many ways it could fail and perhaps be very painful for the parents and for them. And yet, deep down, I knew that this opportunity to be acknowledged and accepted publicly by our parents and friends is something each of the men longed for and that I, too, needed.

There is a Japanese term, called "death by overwork," which I believe has a lot to do with the need of Asian men to overachieve because they are starving for acknowledgment and don't know how to ask for it. In so many ways, White society and the Asian culture don't make it easy or safe to ask for acknowledgment. Asian men are often seen as insecure or self-centered if they express what they need emotionally, such as wanting to be listened to, needing to be told they are doing well, or being acknowledged publicly.

Often, the only time we honor someone's achievements is when he or she is dead or retiring. There is really only one time in our lives that we are totally accepted, and that is when we are babies. We don't have to do anything or be anything to be loved—just ourselves. What a great beginning and what a tremendous letdown it must be to never have that kind of acceptance and acknowledgment again. I believe this hunger and loss of acceptance are the roots of a lot of anger and violence. Often men who are violent have poor self-esteem and feel powerless and unaccepted in their relationships.

As a way of involving them, the parents and friends are asked to bring something to eat or to drink. The reason for this is because, in the Asian culture, bringing food to someone's house is considered a way of thanking the host and honoring the invitation. We encourage some of the guests that were a bit shy to begin opening up by sharing with someone else what they had made and maybe swap some recipes. Food is such a universal bridge for creating friendships and understanding.

Another exchange we do is pairing folks up with someone they haven't met before and asking them to introduce each other. Sometimes they're asked to share with the group the origin of their names. More recently, they were asked to talk about something they've never shared with anyone. We do this to illustrate the art and gift of listening as well as to create a situation for each person to relate with someone new safely and equally.

Acknowledgment Ceremony Stories

During the ceremony one of the Asian men who had been divorced for many years had his 8-year-old son turn to him and say, "Dad, I don't want you to go away again. I want you to stay home and play with me while I grow up. I love you, Daddy." They both hugged and cried. The father later shared that he never knew that this decision to leave the area reminded his son of the time he left his family when they divorced. He also didn't know how important it was for his son that his father be there while he grew up. For a long time the father had lived with the shame of having left his family for another woman. He had never quite forgiven himself. His major issue in the group was with commitment and shame. The ceremony was the first step in a renewed relationship with his family and his children, as well as an important beginning in feeling good about himself as a father and as a man.

Another father shared that he wished he had a group like this when he was growing up because he might have been a better father. He also shared that his father never really talked to him and that he wanted it to be different between his son and him. At the end he hugged his son and told him how much he loved him.

There was a Japanese father who stood up and shared that ever since he came to this country he had never used his Japanese name in public. On this night, he shared with us his Japanese name, and there were tears of pride in his eyes as we cried in happiness with him.

These are only a few of the many touching stories that have been told over the past 5 years that have opened our hearts and moved everyone who came. The acknowledgment ceremony has created a space and an opportunity for the parents to give to their sons what they might have longed for from their parents. As for the Asian men, the ceremony has been chance to hear from their friends and parents the gift of acceptance and acknowledgment so that they can feel empowered and good about themselves.

ISSUES OF RACISM

The issue of racism has a tremendous impact on the Asian American community. Racism in America toward Asians is on the rise and continues to cause a great deal of anguish and pain, even death. To deal with the issue of violence and anger, one must always include racism as a major cause.

When I started the Asian Men's Group in 1985, I attempted to begin with the issue of racism, but I found that the men quickly turned to issues affecting their personal lives, such as girlfriends and family pressures. Why was that? Were they afraid of confronting their ethnicities? Were there too much anger and pain?

As the months progressed, I realized that they were asking me to take them to a different place, one that they hadn't shared with anyone else—a journey through their personal history. What they were asking for was for everyone to share their most intimate secrets and relationships, including me. To them, this was a way of testing the safety and trustworthiness of the group. Over the years, each man realized that this group had become his second family, in many ways, more accepting and more intimate than any family he had ever experienced; that week after week, no matter how difficult it got in the group, no one would leave or abandon him.

When we finally dealt with the issue of racism, we were faced with a great deal of internalized racism. "Internalized racism" is a term that is used to describe the perpetuation by an individual of stereotypes that have been developed about his or her particular ethnic group. For example, when an Asian American woman won't date Asian American men because she has heard that they are wimps, lacking in passion, sexist, and passive, she has "internalized" White society's stereotypes of Asian American men. To break this internalized racism, psychodrama and self-disclosure exercises were used in the group, as well as validation and acknowledgment.

RACISM WORKSHOP

Psychodrama is a powerful tool in reliving a racist experience. If the environment is safe and honest enough, the experience can be used to can reenact the pain and anguish. The men in the group created a role play in which a Japanese man was double parked and a White man drives up and gets out of his car, swearing and using racial epithets.

What came out of the role play was both painful and enlightening. The Japanese man responded to the White man with logic and explanation, trying to appeal to the rational side of the White man. When the Japanese man's explanations failed, he tried to walk away. After the play, the Japanese man explained that, if he had stayed, he probably would have killed the White man.

So often Asian men and men of color share this fear of "killing" the White man if they were to reveal their anger to them. The Asian men in the group expressed that they had never felt safe enough to believe that their anger would be well received or acknowledged by White men, and so they kept their anger inside themselves. In my experience, not once on television or in the movies have I witnessed a White man listening to the anguish and pain of an Asian American man, let alone a White man acknowledging the validity of an Asian American man's anger. What I have seen is White men rescuing Asians, as if they were too weak, emotionally and physically, to help themselves without the powerful, handsome, articulate White American man. My father's childhood stories of winning in a situation were only of how another white man came to his rescue, but never of himself winning the day and never of another Chinese man coming to his aid.

Many of the men in the group deeply identified with the Japanese man in the role play. They shared how humiliated they felt in a similar situation and how they also feared for their lives. The men told about how they felt angry and ashamed of themselves for not having "stood up" and defended themselves, verbally and physically. Racism causes self-hatred and self-mutilation: a mutilation of the Asian American man's image as a powerful and articulate father, warrior, and lover. When that kind of emotional destruction is passed on from one generation to another in the form of warnings from our fathers to watch out for the White man and limitations on the type of careers we can pursue, then it degrades and diminishes the community and its potential to develop powerful leaders.

The Asian men in the group related how their fathers told them to plan for the future, to postpone any kind of anger they were feeling now. They were told to go to college and to get a good-paying job. My father used to say, "When you have a good home and a good job, then the White men will have to look up at you. For now, let them call you names. How can that hurt you? They are only stupid. You know who you are." The trouble I had with my father's statement was that, at 12 years old, I didn't know who I was. I think my father was afraid and unsure of himself at my age too, but later pride and shame kept him from revealing that part of himself to his sons. I also think that Asian fathers warn their children to be careful and to avoid trouble, because they want to protect them from disappointment and racist responses. However, the problem with this type of postponement is that if you don't get the great education or the great home in the suburbs, does that mean that you're not as good as the White man? Or if you do get a good education and have a good house, does that mean you won't experience racism?

The man who played the part of the White man was ecstatic at the amount of rage and racism he could express. Yelling at the top of his voice without the fear of reprisal and being able to threaten bodily harm were just two of the new emotions he felt. He was exhilarated and overwhelmed at the extent of power being a White man encompassed. The use of the White mask was helpful because he felt like a "new person" removed from his usual cultural restraints of honor and modesty. Also, the mask hid his emotions, so he could just rely on his voice and body gestures. The mask was appropriate because the men in the group often talked about how "unfeeling and invulnerable" Whites looked when they called them racist names. With the mask, this man could hide his uncertainty—he could be cruel and outrageous without any emotional limitation. There are ample models of White men reacting out of control and full of rage on television and at the movies that the Asian man could imitate but, as usual, very few Asian models with the same kind of emotions.

To heal the pain of feeling humiliated, the Japanese man who played the victim in the role play was encouraged to talk about what he had "lost" in this experience and the grief he felt at not being able to fully express the rage and humiliation. What came up for the other men in the group were feelings of being unsupported and invalidated in their own lives when they told their White friends about what had happened to them during a racist experience. Some of the reasons their White friends gave for racist remarks were that the White man was probably having a "bad day at work," the Asian man probably misunderstood what the White person said, or the incident didn't really happen. The men in the group also told of other cases, where the White person who was listening related about worst cases of racism he had heard of, thereby diminishing the Asian American man's experience. I remember when I told a White counselor about a painful racist experience, she started to tell me about a similar experience she had gone through. When she finished, I felt somehow obligated to take care of her. In any case, I felt that my story was not as important as hers, even though somehow her experience was supposed to make me feel better.

The dilemma facing Asian men is that if they tell someone else what happened to them, they are often invalidated. If the Asian men don't say anything they are left to "swallow their anger" and to feel ashamed. No wonder our fathers protected us. An Asian man to express his anger was often in a no-win situation. The purpose of the Asian Men's Group is to support each man in "reclaiming" his power and rightful place in American society by listening and validating his experience. Notice that I use *reclaim*, not the word *empower*. To reclaim means that Asian Americans always had what they were told was missing in them, they need only reclaim their power. For example, White America portrays Asian Americans as passive and inarticulate, while in fact they may be merely listening and waiting for an opportunity to speak. This differs from empower, which connotes that power needs to be given.

Recently, the Asian men talked about what they had lost because of racism. They talked about losing their sense of pride, safety, and powerfulness. They also shared a loss of seeing people as individuals. Now they viewed people as "ethnic groups," not as individuals. One of the men said, "Not only did I lose my trust of other people, but I also lost trust in myself. I no longer felt as self-assured and confident. I felt more guarded and watchful." Another Asian man related, "I lost my sense of commonness with other people, that we were all alike. I realized I couldn't walk into North Carolina without feeling defensive and isolated." A Chinese American man in the group said, "What I lost was this sense that my dreams had no boundaries. I lost my feeling of being accepted and having pride in myself. Now I felt I was in competition with other groups for acceptance by Whites."

What the Asian Men's Group offers a survivor of racism is a chance to grieve about his loss and his betrayal, his anguish and his shame. This is important, because the group validates that indeed something did happen, something horrible and unjust was done. These "reality statements" are necessary to help with the giving process because when an act of betrayal occurs, being able to trust someone else to hear your story and to believe you is essential to feeling safe again. So often as American men, we are told to avoid grief and to keep a "stiff upper lip" and to "hold up our end." But the grieving process is necessary to the anger process. Often anger is not our first emotion. Many times we get angry because our hurt is not seen or validated. When our hurt is acknowledged, so is our anger. However, I think that in the case of Asian American men, when their anger is not validated or safe to express, they feel sure that their hurt will not be, either.

In our group, after the grieving process has started, the survivor of racism has the opportunity to "reclaim" what he has lost. He does this by declaring in front of the whole group what he wants back. He can also choose to reenter the role play and act out what he wanted to say and do the first time. When he finishes what he needs to say, he is then acknowledged and validated by the White man in the role play. Having a second try at something we have failed at or feel ashamed about is very rare in life. So what the group offers the men is a chance to reframe their past, to complete their anger, to feel validated and acknowledged, to "reclaim" their power.

In 1991 I wrote a poem, that best describes my "reclaiming" of my birth name and all the other things that I felt that White America had me feel that I was missing. I dedicated the poem to my father and my grandfather whose courage and perseverance inspired me to reclaim my birthright to be honored and respected for who I am.

Bok Fan

I never knew that my eyes were not as opened as yours
that the color of my skin was yellow
that these words I spoke were harsh and foreign.

I always thought that this land of my birth
this place were I took my first breath
was the same as yours.

When I was young, I thought we both ate hom yeur ging gee yook,
bok fan, see you guy and lop cheung
The same as any family coming home from work.

I did not know that my foods were strange or smelled
Just as I never knew my quietness would be seen as weak
My waiting, a sign that I was empty and without fire.

I was taught that waiting was a sign of virtue and an honor
And that the eyes and heart were more direct than words.

But I have learned; you do not follow the path of my hands
or hear the words of my eyes.

You do not smell the sweet fire of the blackbean
or lower your eyes to honor the old ones.

Instead, you speak over my words
Call me "little" as if I were a child

Decide that I cannot sing the sweet songs of love
or hold a woman with my tenderness alone.

You have stolen the dragon's fire from my father's lips
And now you seek to rob me of a warrior's life.

Do you not see the blood that you have spilled
or the children you have shamed?

See me now.
My name is Lee Mun Wah. My name is Lee Mun Wah.

CONCLUSION

How to deal with anger in the Asian American community is not only complex, but also difficult to understand because there is so little information available or groups working on this issue. The Asian Men's Group that I founded in 1985 is a 6-year-study about six men, of which four are from the original group. what I have written is only a small glimpse of some of the many issues and feelings that Asian American men are experiencing today. Nonetheless, the work in this group is important because it represents a way of working with Asian American men that has helped create choices in the ways that they can express their anger and feel validated and powerful. It has also shown how their families have affected how they dealt with anger and how racism creates and reinforces self-hatred and distrust of others.

One of the challenges for Asian Americans is the issue of assimilation—to decide for ourselves what part of the American culture works for us and which part is demeaning and insulting to our heritage. As Asian Americans, we need to also sift through our Asian culture and embrace what is meaningful, useful, and necessary for our self-esteem and identity without feeling compromised or ashamed. The difficult work that lies ahead is how to bring our "blended selves" into mainstream America to be seen and accepted as passionate, powerful, and articulate Asian Americans. Until that time comes, there needs to be places and ways in which Asian Americans can safely express their anger and hurt in safe and validating environments.

Epilogue
Jerry Tello

It is the belief of indigenous people of all roots that we are part of a larger story and that each of us has a role to play and a lesson to teach. Life is a duality and carries with it both the beautiful and the painful lessons. The painful part of the lesson that we have focused on is that of family violence and the men that struggle with this imbalance. It is the responsibility of all of us because we know it not only hurts the victim but the offender and the interconnected web of people that make up the family and human circle.

In truth, the task of presenting a reflection of this issue and its implications was no easy journey, but one that needed to be traveled and explored. Not that the knowledge and experience is not present but attempting to find "the way" to convey the necessary teachings in a respectful and honorable manner was a lesson in itself. It took a total of *seven* years to complete this circle, a number that is held sacred in many traditions. Along the path there were many obstacles, lessons, and blessings that accompanied us. The authors attempted to share their knowledge and experience in a respectful way with an eye towards balancing the traditional indigenous teachings and that of Western contemporary theory and practice. The result is a reflection of teachings and challenges for all of us to discuss while searching for the interconnected healing for all involved.

In this volume Robert Hampton, Ph.D. and Ricardo Carrillo, Ph.D. set the foundation by reminding us that "Americans of minority status are at greater risk of victimization by violent crime than those of majority status." More specifically, they bring into context the issue of race as a significant factor.

> Within this context, all types of violence in communities of color are a public health and criminal justice issue . . . African Americans . . . suffer disproportionately from preventable diseases and deaths; that without the

willingness to deal with race, we cannot make headway in dealing with crime in this country (p. 2).

They go on to suggest that some studies reveal that marital violence may be partially due to these historical experiences of institutional racism, integrated oppression, and colonialism. Finally, they substantiate the lack of culturally competent literature, research, and treatment models in the areas of family violence and men of color.

In the subsequent chapters that focus on the Latino population, Carrillo and Dr. Jerry Tello demonstrate the significance of culturally syntonic aspects of theory and intervention processes. Through the discussion and use of narrative processing (storytelling), cultural indigenous teachings, ceremony, ritual, and traditional healing, they stress the significance of identity and culture and the integrated impact of colonialism and multi generational oppression. Through the utilization of a story, Tello lays the groundwork for seeing family violence within the context of young men lost on the journey to manhood. He further reveals in "The Bridge Story" the multigenerational lessons that are never learned by some while attempting to cross the bridge to maturity thus leading to wounded men with false lessons. He then challenges us to consider the re-traumatization that occurs daily to victims and offenders by stating

> We see how it becomes necessary to not only address the imbalanced violent behavior that is a symptom of a deeper self-denigrating spiritual identity violation but to address it in the context of the total past and present sociohistorical oppression (p. 46).

Carrillo and Goubaud begin the next chapter by stressing the importance of family in the treatment of domestic violence. He states, "The end result of the present day system appears to have essentially taken the 'family' out of family violence." He offers a culturally-based treatment process that combines clinical treatment with indigenous culturally-sensitive healing practices. Then, as echoed by all the other authors, Carillo speaks to the impact of European colonialization on Latino men.

> Latino men are traditionally socialized to protect their family and the paradox is that after several periods of colonialization they have become the oppressor in their own home (p. 58).

It is his premise that domestic violence in the Latino male population has its roots in European colonialization. Dr. Carrillo gives specific examples of the significance and the use of ceremony, spirituality, symbols, music and metaphors. "The use of these cultural processes allows for the unfreezing of the dysfunctional thoughts and behaviors that contribute to the violence." Finally he speaks to the importance for lifelong healing in the need for a culturally-based support group of men (compadres) that are not afraid to reject violence in their communities.

Dr. Oliver Williams begins the next chapter with an allegory depicting the African American male as an endangered species. The healthy individual "tend[s] to flourish in environments that match their capabilities" (p. 74).

In this chapter Dr. Williams examines the inordinate amount of stressors that African American men have historically faced and continue to face just to maintain their purpose or "rhythm" in life. Williams, in this chapter, challenges the conventional explanation of domestic violence as merely based in gender equality and man's attempt to maintain control. He states

> The intersection of race, social status and violence creates a set of issues that have typically not been discussed in the literature on domestic violence . . . before we can truly understand violence perpetrated by African American males there must be a critique of the African American man's experience in the United States (pp. 77, 79).

Truly this view would dictate a much larger scope of training, understanding, and development for anyone wanting to treat African American offenders. Williams goes on to outline his philosophy and the basis for addressing effectively the issue of domestic violence and the African American male.

> A common philosophy should include the following points: violent men must be held accountable for their behavior; there is no justification for male violence; violent men must learn to negotiate life challenges, alternatives to controlling and reducing their sexist attitudes and behavior. . . . At first glance it might appear an enriched perspective retains the beliefs presently held in the field of partner abuse. It differs, though, because African American male perspectives must be included as ingredients which shape the treatment content and design (p. 84).

He concludes by quoting Robert Allen

> Black men must hold each other responsible for challenging sexism in our community as we challenge the racism of White America . . . at the Million Man March disavowing wife abuse, abuse of children and the use of misogynist language was an affirming and healing gesture (p. 91).

In the next chapter, Duran and others guide us through an in-depth understanding of a postcolonial perspective on domestic violence in Indian country. Woodis begins by sharing a dream narrative that extends the view that domestic violence is reflective of "caging" the spirit of the Indian culture. In a field that has virtually ignored the Indian population in research and treatment the authors offer insightful and relevant knowledge and experience. They urge the additional focus needed for the Indian population by stating

> Through the collective clinical and community work that the authors have been doing for over 20 years it is safe to say that there is at least as much domestic violence in Indian country as there is in the rest of society (p. 97).

On the same note they emphasize the need for culturally relevant models.

> Many of the models for treatment are based on western interventions. Imposing these models of intervention on Indian people would merely perpetrate another form of violence and further colonialization on our community. . . . By this we mean that they partake in ideological/cultural domination by the assertion of universality and neutrality and by the disavowal of all other cultural forms or interpretations (p. 97).

In a continued criticism of conventional interventions the authors share

> Many of the approaches that pretend to heal the pain of domestic violence instead seek someone to victimize and blame. They too concur with other authors in this book as they speak to the effects of oppression (p. 98).

Recent literature clearly demonstrates how historical trauma continues to manifest itself in all types of unhealthy behavior patterns across Indian country. Within the internalized oppression paradigm the male dynamics have a specific expression:

> The Lakota wicasa, or man, was robbed of his traditional role as hunter, protector, and provider. He lost his status and honor. This negatively impacted his relationship with Lakota women and children. A further assault on the Lakota and all Indian people was the prohibition against indigenous spiritual practices in 1883 (p. 100).

Later in this chapter they offer an indigenous based framework to view and treat domestic violence. This profound insight allows us to expand our perception of domestic violence from an indigenous perspective.

> If you are a male a female stands within you; if you are a female a male stands within you. In offering pollen in prayer in this manner a balance in soul and a balance in nature is sustained and maintained. This balancing ritual between the two life forces of male and female serves to remind both of the interrelationship and respect for each other (p. 108).

In the final chapters, Dr. Tong and Mun Wah look into Asian men and domestic violence. Dr. Tong begins by retelling a traditional story of a female warrior. By way of this narrative he sets forth the challenges of maintaining one's cultural traditions in an ever-changing Westernized world. Tong continues by offering his perspective that

> The etiological roots of domestic abuse—whether physical, emotional or sexual—are to be found in four interrelated phenomena: problems of adaptation, cross-cultural clashes, racist oppression, and repressive heritage (p. 116).

He goes on to stress the importance of culture in one's view and behavior in the world.

> A people's deepest beliefs and world views or mythos, provides for a coherent narrative to address three fundamental concerns that cut across collective existence as well as individual lives: (1) history, a sense of the past, or who we have always been; (2) identity, a sense of the present or who were or should be right now; and (3) destiny, a sense of the present, or who are or should be. . . . Events like war, economic chaos or natural disasters disrupt the substance and continuity of all three. . . . Long before an Asian American abuses spouse or children, she/he have already suffered flagrant and wholesale abuse (p. 117).

Finally, he leaves us with the importance of considering migration and its effects.

> Coupled with the adaptational demands of migration and the conflicts resulting from the clash of White cultural domination, these powerful forces have shaped the special arena within which Asian American domestic violence, in all its forms, is played out (p. 124).

The second author in this section, Lee Mun Wah, continues the discussion of these issues utilizing a narrative flow to reveal the personal nature of domestic violence and healing. In a personal reflection he offers,

> One day I got really mad at one of the men in the group. One of the other men said he thought *I wasn't being angry enough*. I was furious—I told him for an Asian man that I was really angry. . . . What I learned was that working through anger is not something that can be taught in isolation or without the recognition of one's cultural background (pp. 129–130).

Mun Wah gives us insight not only into anger and Asian men but how important tne cultural influences are. "None of the Asian men in the group had ever witnessed anger being resolved in their families." He continues by reflecting the needs of Asian men in dealing with domestic violence.

> I came to realize after a few weeks that each of the men in the group needed something from myself and the rest of the group that they weren't getting from their families or their communities—acknowledgment and support to explore their fears, their anger, their relationships, their hurt, their dreams and their desires (p. 130).

From here on he guides the process and the thinking behind working with Asian men and domestic violence. He concludes by stating

> What I see is the need for American culture to respect and not to judge that other cultures that are different, are inferior. . . . How we choose to see the world determines how the world sees us (p. 135).

CONCLUSION

This writing was more than an exercise in theoretical formulation—it was a journey of dialogue, prayer, ceremony and healing. Authors from various roots concurred on several important points.

1. The field is sorely lacking in research and treatment models to assist in the healing of men of color and domestic violence.

2. The present models not only are not adequate but many times mirror the violence and control that we are attempting to address.

3. A major root cause of domestic violence and men of color is in the historical oppression and violence that people of color have experienced and continue to experience today.

4. Spirituality is a foundational element needed in the assessment and healing processes in working with men of color.

5. The integrated inclusion of family/community as part of the healing and ongoing recovery process is essential.

In the traditional way we end as we began by acknowledging that we the authors are merely messengers (of the creator) of healing and learning. We attempted in no way to purport ourselves as the experts. We have offered not the final word but just another perspective to encourage the dialogue. With this in mind we apologize if through this process we have offended. In a consistent manner with the teachings we offer men in the healing process we take full reponsibility for what we have shared. Our hope is and has always been that what we have offered can contribute in a positive way towards the healing of all people so that the children and the subsequent generations can live in a world filled with peace, harmony, and an affirmed purpose in life.

The elders share that many of us have lived through seven generations of pain and it will take seven generations to heal, so we must start now.

CON CARIÑO Y RESPETO

Index